Foreword

The city of 100 towers, the golden city, the magical city, the mother of all cities, the little mother with claws: for centuries, nicknames have been given to the Czech capital in attempts to describe its character. Its beauty, its history and its unmistakeable atmosphere have always drawn masses of visitors. The city library has its own *Praguensia* department. Thousands of pages in books and blogs have been written about Prague, and a host of tour guides and agencies have specialised in individual aspects of the city – from its Functionalist architecture to the places connected with corruption.

Anyone who wants to add one more piece to the mosaic has to face the question of what is unique about their new contribution. Our answer is that, on the one hand, we want to draw attention to places that have been forgotten by most tour guides and also by many citizens of Prague, and on the other to make the selection as diverse as possible. That's why we're sending you to a strudel maker as well as a police museum, to a statue with a Cubist canopy and a bicycle tour through concrete tower blocks, to an exhibition in what used to be a Nazi torture dungeon, and also to a pub surrounded by allotments.

These places have been chosen for the benefit of everyone, from inquisitive newcomers to old hands in the city. The former will discover something new, the latter a fascinating detail or an unaccustomed perspective. It goes without saying that this choice of places is subjective, and that there are not merely 111 places in Prague that you shouldn't miss, but many, many more. If this book inspires you to take a look at the spots and districts that we invite you to visit, and also to discover further places, we will feel doubly honoured.

111 Places

Matěj Černý and Marie Peřinová

111 Places in Prague That You Shouldn't Miss

emons:

© Emons Verlag GmbH
All rights reserved
© for photographs: Matěj Černý, Marie Peřinová, except
BoysPlayNice (place 107); Česká spořitelna, a. s. (place 79);
Michal Čížek (places 1, 3, 4, 7, 8, 11, 20, 25, 30, 31, 32, 34, 37, 44,
45, 49, 55, 59, 60, 61, 63, 68, 71, 73, 91, 94, 102, 106, 109, 111);
Jan Hrdý, Corrupt Tour (place 19); Pragulic (place 74);
Tomáš Souček, MeetFactory (place 56)
© Cover motif: fotolia.com/Roman Vukolov
English translation: John Sykes
Editors: Tizian Books
Design: Eva Kraskes, based on a design
by Lübbeke | Naumann | Thoben
Maps: altancicek.design, www.altancicek.de
Printing and binding: Hitzegrad Print Medien & Service –
Lensing Druck Gruppe, Feldbachacker 16, 44149 Dortmund
Printed in Germany 2017
ISBN 978-3-7408-0144-1

Did you enjoy it? Do you want more?
Join us in uncovering new places around the world on:
www.111places.com

1 007 Music Club

The underground legend of Strahov

Some people think that "Strahov Seven" is overshadowed by bigger venues that are closer to the city centre. And besides, they say, it's no more than a student club. Nevertheless, the name of this club is music to the ears of acoustic gourmets – and not just metaphorically, since the sound engineer has worked here for 25 years and has true cult status.

No club has played a more important role in the Czech music scene. 007 started out in 1969 in the cellar of a student hall of residence in the Technical University. This means that it's Prague's oldest music club with a continuous existence. Its history also reflects the succession of musical styles that were seen as alternative in their time. In the late 1960s and early 1970s folk singers played here. Later came jazz-rock, disco, new wave, underground and punk. Theatre was performed, films were screened and, in spite of pressure from the regime, the students who ran the joint succeeded in maintaining its relatively free character.

In 1987 one of them was Ivo Kučera. He still runs the club today – and this makes him as much a legend as "his" Klub 007 itself. Perhaps the intimate atmosphere is the reason: the room only has space for 180 people. Or is it the remarkable energy of the place, which has always been a draw for innovative bands? The club rents out its space directly to concert organisers. In this way it became a stronghold of fans of hardcore, though today there is a diverse mixture of genres. Bands with a modest fan base perform, but also musicians who could be among the top acts at the Glastonbury Festival in a few years – the British band the xx, for example.

However, your personal highlight at the club might also be a concert by a band that could break up soon afterwards. As Ivo Kučera puts it, "A visit to a club is always a one-off experience. You never know how it'll turn out."

Address Chaloupeckého 1915/7, 169 00 Prague 6, www.klub007strahov.cz | **Getting there** Metro B to Karlovo náměstí, then bus 176 to Strahov stadium; go past the stadium to the other student hall of residence | **Hours** Sun – Thu 7pm – midnight, Fri & Sat 7pm – 1am; concerts end at 10pm on the dot | **Tip** If you get hungry at Strahov and you're there before 8.30pm (or 7.30pm on Fridays or Saturdays), go to the student dining hall in Jezdecká. The prices are student level and the quality is OK.

2__Ad for the Liberated Theatre

Braying donkeys and other politicians

"Daily performances." This advertising slogan would tempt no one out of their warm living room today, even if it covered the side of a whole building. However, it's still interesting, even though – or possibly because – the theatre ensemble concerned has long ceased to exist.

Since 2009 the 80-year-old outdoor advertisement for the Liberated Theatre and its famous duo of comedians, Jan Werich and Jiří Voskovec, has been visible again, restored by the city authorities. It's a little hidden away, on an end wall in a courtyard in the street V Jámě, right next to the U Nováků building, to which the avant-garde ensemble moved in 1930. Today this stage is home to Divadlo ABC, but it was once the place where Voskovec and Werich treated audiences to their humorous performances.

After the Nazis took power in Germany, they became more and more political. In the original version of the skit called *Donkeys and Shadows*, the authentic voice of Adolf Hitler rang out from the donkey's mouth. Later, the voice and the name of the figure had to be changed, for diplomatic reasons. The song *Tmavomodrý svět* by the jazz composer Jaroslav Ježek, who worked closely with the comedy duo, was premiered in this theatre, along with other hits.

The advertising on the wall includes caricatures of Voskovec and Werich created by Adolf Hoffmeister, an artist who collaborated closely with the Liberated Theatre. He employed less garish colours than are usual in advertising today, mainly ochre and grey, as in those days it was easier to attract the attention of passers-by. It is precisely this understatement that makes the advertisement special. It's a pity that such elegant memories of the interwar period in Czechoslovakia, company signs or advertisements, are disappearing from the urban scene – even though many cafés are promoting the atmosphere of this era.

Address V Jámě – near Štěpánská, 110 00 Prague 1 | **Getting there** Tram 3, 5, 6, 9, 14, 24 to Vodičkova, or metro A, B to Můstek (exit to Václavské náměstí) | **Tip** If you're interested in photography, at Školská 28 you'll find a little gem, the Leica Gallery, and a pleasant café. Up to seven annual exhibitions presenting the work of top Czech, Slovak and international photographers are held here, and you can take part in workshops.

3 Anděl Metro Station
Underground communism

You can normally recognise Prague's metro stations by the colour of their walls. At Anděl, it's worth looking more closely: between the expanses of marble cladding, on each side there are four bronze reliefs depicting bouquets of flowers, ears of wheat, cosmonauts and fluttering flags. Welcome to the world of "Czech-Soviet friendship."

Until 1990 Anděl metro station was called Moskevská – a classic example of communist brotherhood. It was built by Soviet architects and artists while their Czech colleagues were adorning the Pražskaya station in Moscow. The two underground stops were opened almost simultaneously in 1985. The artists were given the task of designing the stations in the style of their own country, so in Prague traditional Soviet themes were illustrated – "Success in Agriculture, Aviation and World Peace," for example. If you take the exit towards Knížecí, you'll pass a bronze sculpture marked with the words "Moskva – Praha." The similarity to Russian metro stations is so striking that in 2015 Anděl was used for a scene in the film *Child 44*, which is set in the Soviet Union.

In the 1990s it was still possible to feel you were in the Soviet Union even outside the metro: a stone mosaic in the entrance hall depicts a panorama of Moscow, and a grey district of abandoned buildings and old factories used to extend around the station. Today, vibrant urban life welcomes the visitor: modern office buildings and a shopping centre. In 2000 the metro entrance was incorporated into the Golden Angel complex of buildings, designed by the French architect Jean Nouvel.

The reliefs above the metro platforms were also nearly destroyed after the Velvet Revolution. They were gone for a period of several months, and then suddenly reappeared in their usual position. The transport authority seemingly decided that communism had already obliterated enough history.

Address Anděl metro station, 150 00 Prague 5 | Getting there Metro B | Hours Daily
5am−midnight | Tip Take a close look at the glass façade of the Golden Angel building to
see quotes in Czech from the works of Franz Kafka, Rainer Maria Rilke, Gustav Meyrink
and other authors who wrote in and about Prague, and also an image, more or less distinct
depending on the light, of an angel, inspired by Wim Wenders' film *Wings of Desire*.

4 Bad Fingers

From a different angle

You don't always have to go out to the edge of Prague, or search for obscure spots in the city centre, to discover something new. Even the best-known places in the city can surprise you. All you have to do is look at things from a different angle. It's enough to take a few steps to one side, and a sculpture changes its dignified posture. Try it for yourself, keeping one eye closed.

On the Old Town side of the Charles Bridge you can see the famous statue of Charles IV. In his right hand, the emperor is holding the Golden Bull which he issued – the most important constitutional document of the Holy Roman Empire. That is the usual view. Now take a look at the monument from the corner of Křižovnická ulice and Křižovnické náměstí square, with the Church of St Francis on the right. The great document of state, of all things, that the emperor was holding in his hand a moment ago, now appears to show him carrying out one of the most banal human activities – you might be reminded of the "Manneken Pis" in Brussels.

Whereas Charles IV was known to the Czechs as "Father of the Homeland," the man who was the first president of Czechoslovakia from 1918 to 1935, Tomáš Garrigue Masaryk, also received a patriarchal nickname: the people called him "Papa Masaryk." Czechs often simply call him TGM. Everyone knows his statue on the Hradčany.

When the sculptors represented this philosopher-president in a statesmanlike pose of debate, they didn't realise that, from a certain angle, Masaryk's right hand would look like the claws of a crab. To see this, take up a position with your back to the archbishop's palace. The "right" point of view is to look at the statue from the imagined straight line that connects the left-hand door of the palace with the locked door on the left that leads into the castle grounds. And now you really need to use your imagination.

Address Charles IV: Křižovnické náměstí, 110 00 Prague 1; T. G. Masaryk: Hradčanské náměstí, 118 00 Prague 1 | **Getting there** Charles IV: Tram 17, 18 to Karlovy lázně; T. G. Masaryk: Tram 22 to Pohořelec | **Tip** There is a copy of the statue of Masaryk in Mexico City, on the main shopping street which bears his name: Avenida Presidente Tomás Garrigue Masaryk.

5   The Barrandov Terraces
Prague Functionalism as Sleeping Beauty

Authors never want their work to go out of date quickly. In the case of the Barrandov Terraces, by contrast, we couldn't wish for anything more keenly. What is today a paradise for urban explorers investigating dilapidated buildings not open to the public was a popular place in the interwar period: when the weather was good, the people of Prague came here in their thousands – not only for meals in the French restaurant and the unrivalled view of Prague, but also to get a glimpse of film stars making movies in the nearby studios, who came over for a quick visit.

In 1926 Václav M. Havel, father of the Czech president, had the Terraces built on a rock above the Vltava. The centrepiece of the ensemble was a Functionalist-style restaurant, with a viewing tower whose silhouette rose above tables with sunshades. In summer the tables filled several levels. A swimming pool lower down near the Vltava, today as shabby as the rest of the buildings, was also part of the complex.

In 1948 the Terraces were nationalised. From that time on they fell into decay. Without the necessary maintenance they crumbled, and in 1989 they were returned to the Havel family in a desolate condition. Their fate is said to have pained the president greatly, but he failed to find an investor. There was no profit in renovating the two garden restaurants, particularly because of the permanent traffic noise from several main roads. Havel's family sold the terraces in 2003.

Although the new owner planned to restore the site, which had protected status, and convert it into a hotel, the only new life there came in the form of sprouting weeds and a few homeless people. In spring 2016, however, workers finally appeared to clear away the bushes. So perhaps the Terraces will be restored to their original condition in due course. Until then: have you ever considered doing some urban exploration?

Address Barrandovská 165/1, 152 00 Prague 1 | **Getting there** Metro B to Smíchovské nádraží, then bus 105 to Terasy. Opposite the bus stop go into Barrandovská, then take a path through the bushes on the left after a few metres | **Hours** Officially no access – you enter explicitly at your own risk | **Tip** A walk of about one kilometre, through a once-famous district of villas, takes you to Kříženeckého náměstí, where the main building of the film studio is situated. At weekends you can see the Filmpoint exhibition, which is dedicated to the classic movies *Three Gifts for Cinderella* and *Amadeus*.

6 Behind Monastery Walls

Stay in the Capuchin monastery on the castle hill

Heavy wooden boards creak beneath your feet as you tread on them. You can sometimes hear singing when you pass the refectory. Perhaps one of the many doors might open, and you will be greeted quietly by one of the students who live here. Then press down the latch, and you'll find yourself in your modestly but tastefully furnished room. Welcome to the Capuchin monastery on the Hradčany, one of the most interesting places for an overnight stay in Prague.

For an incredibly cheap 400 Kč (300 Kč if you bring your own sleeping bag) you can spend the night here. But the price is not the main thing – it's the atmosphere that counts. The monastery is neither a hotel nor a hostel. Although there are a few dormitories for school groups, most of the rooms have just one to three beds. You don't have to share them with strangers, but neither can you expect the classic services of a hotel. The Wi-Fi works without a hitch, but the toilets and showers are shared facilities reached via the corridor. Breakfast is not provided, and you have to make your own bed. To make up for this, you are, with a little luck, treated to the sight of the monks in their hoods, and views of the lanes of the picturesque Nový Svět quarter.

The monastery was built in the early 17th century. In 1757 it was damaged by the Prussian army, and cannonballs from that time can still be seen in the wall of the church. In 1944 the SS converted it into a prison for German deserters, and in April 1945 the monastery received a letter from the Third Reich promising compensation – as soon as Germany had won the war. The communists who took over later lacked this sense of humour. They imprisoned the monks, and converted the monastery into the headquarters of the counterespionage service. Now the monastery is again in the hands of the Capuchin monks, who carefully restored it in the 1990s.

Address Klášter kapucínů, Loretánské náměstí 6a, 118 00 Prague 1; at www.kapucini.cz click "Ubytování v Praze" on the left and select the English version | **Getting there** Tram 22 to Pohořelec, then walk 450 metres | **Hours** Room keys can be collected up to 4pm, or later if arranged by telephone. | **Tip** For excellent coffee from the Prague coffee roaster Doubleshot or a light meal, go to the café Nový Svět in the alley of that name. It is one of the few tourist-free places in this part of the city.

7 Bertha's Memorial Plaque

Lay Down Your Arms!

How many Czech Nobel Prize laureates do you know? The writer Jaroslav Seifert? The physical chemist Jaroslav Heyrovský? Some might also mention Václav Havel or Otto Wichterle, the inventor of the contact lens, even though neither of these two won the prize. In a niche in the Kinský Palace on Old Town Square there hangs a memorial plaque with a relief and a name that has been practically forgotten in the Czech Republic. The initiator of the peace movement, Bertha von Suttner, spent her early childhood here. She was the first woman to receive the Nobel Prize for Peace, in 1905.

From the 18th century the extensive residence belonged to the Kinský family, an ancient Bohemian aristocratic dynasty.

However, young Bertha did not live here long. Her father Franz Kinský died before her birth, and as her mother didn't come from a noble family, the rest of the Kinskýs looked down on her and her child. Soon Bertha was living in Brno, then in Vienna, and finally she moved to Georgia with her husband, Arthur von Suttner. Here she worked in military hospitals during the Russo-Turkish War and became a pacifist. The result of this was a famous anti-war novel, *Lay Down Your Arms*.

For a short time Bertha von Suttner was the secretary of Alfred Nobel, with whom she had a lifelong friendship. She founded the Austrian Peace Society, and campaigned for the establishment of the International Court of Justice in The Hague. Having warned that the next war would be much worse than all previous ones, she was fortunate not to experience it. She died on 21 June,1914, a week before the assassination of the crown prince of Austria-Hungary. Bertha von Suttner had many critics, some of whom referred to her as "Big Bertha." Paradoxically, the same nickname was given to one of the most fearsome artillery pieces of the World War I – not after her, but after the owner of the Krupp company.

Address Staroměstské náměstí 12, 110 15 Prague 1 | **Getting there** Metro A, B to Můstek, then walk along Na Můstku and Melantrichova to Staroměstské náměstí | **Tip**
In February 1948 a famous photo was taken of President Klement Gottwald speaking to the people from the balcony of the Kinský Palace. On the original photo, Vladimír Clementis, later foreign minister, is standing next to him, but he was later airbrushed out, having been arrested and executed in the struggle against the "enemy within."

8 The Bethlehem Chapel in Žižkov

A Cubist gem in a back yard

When they hear the term Bethlehem Chapel, most people think of Jan Hus and his sermons in the Old Town. Not many realise that there are two chapels of this name in Prague. The less well-known one is not only older, but also has a special feature, in the remarkable survival of its Cubist interior. It's hidden away in the yard of a house with a galleried court in Žižkov, and is thus not even known to all of the neighbours.

In 1914, as the Protestant congregation in the Žižkov district was growing, a decision was made to buy a house on the busy street of Prokopova and to erect a place to worship in its spacious inner courtyard. At that time it was the only Bethlehem chapel in the city, since the church in which Hus preached was demolished in the 18th century and not rebuilt until 1950–52, by the communists, in the form of a monument to the Hussite movement.

The chapel in Žižkov was also in danger of destruction when the far-reaching decision was made for the redevelopment of Žižkov as a socialist estate. But thanks to the pastor, the chapel was given the status of protected heritage in 1975, and thus saved. The interior of this grey building by the architect Emil Králíček is astonishing: it combines elements of Cubism and Art Nouveau. The typical Cubist motif of the star can be seen on the pulpit and beneath the organ. The colourful wall is the work of students from the Academy of Art and dates from 1992. The striking ceiling lights, originally intended for the cathedral of Vyšehrad, are also new.

The chapel is in the care of the Evangelical Church of Bohemian Brethren. For music lovers its attraction goes beyond the organ concerts: a story is doing the rounds that it was a rehearsal room for the Plastic People of the Universe. This is not quite right – the truth is that this is where the band made the acquaintance of their drummer, Jiří Šula.

Address Prokopova 216/4, 130 00 Prague 3 | **Getting there** Metro B, C to Florenc, then bus 133, 175, 207 to Tachovské náměstí | **Hours** No fixed opening times, but accessible to the public. If it's closed, ring the bell at the chapel; a visit can be arranged by contacting the pastor: zizkov1.evangnet.cz | **Tip** On Prokopovo náměstí is the original equestrian statue of Jaroslav Hašek, the author of the legendary *The Good Soldier Švejk*, created by the well-known sculptor Karel Nepraš and his daughter Karolína, who finished the work after her father's death.

9 The Bike Path

A trip to a socialist experiment

Is your idea of a cycle path something like a pleasant route beneath the shade of trees and along a waterway?

If so, the trip from Řepy to Hlubočepy will not disappoint you. It crosses the beautiful Prokop valley, where high slopes flank the stream that gives the valley its name. Make the most of this section, as it's followed by a special experience: riding through Lužiny, a typical huge estate from communist days that is still populated by half a million Prague citizens.

Lužiny was built in the 1970s and 1980s as part of the Jihozápadní město, one of three large-scale housing projects in Prague. The concrete residential blocks are arranged in an unusual way here: circular, with spacious courtyards. Like a long artery, the bike path leads through three such complexes between Píškova in the east and Oistrachova in the west. The main roads where cars drive around the outside of the estates can be crossed on bridges.

The entrance to the estate is a low-roofed passage. It opens on to a large, quiet space with lawns and trees, surrounded by the walls of the residential blocks and hundreds of windows. Whereas residents in the 1980s probably got depressed quite quickly looking out at the grey concrete, today the estates glow in all the colours of the rainbow – thanks to the residents, who try to make them look more human. The courtyards, too, have been renovated. Along with sand pits and kindergartens there are well-equipped playgrounds with rope pyramids and climbing walls.

All the same, there's no escaping the feeling that you're visiting a social experiment: a huge space for living without cafés, shops or galleries, where the only places to meet others are the sand pits on which the residents look down from their apartments every day. So if you don't happen to live on an estate yourself, consider this bike trip to be a kind of educational trail.

Address Cyklostezka Řepy – Hlubočepy, 155 00 Prague 13, www.prazskecyklostezky.cz/cyklostezka/re-hl.aspx | **Getting there** Metro B to Lužiny, then continue on the cycle path. You can make the return journey shorter by taking the metro at Luka station; the route is marked with yellow signs: ŘE–HL. The estate lies between Píškova and Oistrachova streets. | **Tip** If you cross Oistrachova and continue by bike, after a few kilometres you reach the church of St James the Major (Kovářova 21), a Gothic Revival building that was constructed in the early 20th century to replace a Romanesque church. Along with a few other original buildings, the church remains an island in a sea of concrete.

10__Bio Oko

The cinema that should not have been built

For lovers of high-minded cinematography, Prague has a respectable array of art-house cinemas. Bio Oko may not be the oldest cinema, as Ponrepo is; it doesn't have a convenient location in the city centre, like Světozor; and it's not as famous as Aero in Žižkov. Nevertheless, the building alone is definitely worth seeing.

The imposing canopy with the neon lettering *Bio Oko* already suggests that this cinema is a good many years old. The interior fittings, too, go back to the days when people didn't go to multiplexes and rattle boxes of popcorn, but to picture palaces that only had one screen. Yet Bio Oko is not a conserved structure, nor an antique that has had an all-round refurbishment. On the contrary, the first two rows of the auditorium are occupied not by cinema seats, but by beach loungers and padded armchairs dating from the 1970s. For technical reasons it is no longer possible to sit in the Trabant cabriolet, but the management has promised to extend the range of alternative seating soon. There are rumours of a gynaecological chair…

In addition to a broad cinematic programme, Bio Oko is used for exhibitions and various non-traditional activities, such as Sunday brunch with a film. Then the whole of the upper foyer is transformed into a bar, a popular rendezvous for the neighbourhood.

The building of which the cinema is part belongs to a Functionalist block that was constructed in the late 1930s. The designs of the two young architects originally envisaged two separate structures, with the centre left unbuilt. However, an open ensemble was too revolutionary for the city authorities. The building in Františka Křížka, now Bio Oko, was therefore constructed between the other two, creating a closed block. Thus the fact that the cinema exists at all is the result of an unsuccessful rebellion against the architectural conventions of the time.

Address Františka Křížka 15, 170 00 Prague 7, www.biooko.net | **Getting there** Tram 1, 8, 12, 25, 26 to Kamenická, then go along Milady Horákové, and left into Františka Křížka | **Hours** See the cinema programme | **Tip** If you would like to discover another famous café in Letná, go to Bistro 8 at Veverkova 8. Then you can join the debate about whether the quality of the cooking matches the fantastic interior design.

11 Blanka

Have you tunnelled today?

A tunnel is just a hole in the ground, you're going to say. And you're right. Yet Blanka differs from other tunnels in a number of ways.

At 5.5 kilometres, this impressive structure is Europe's longest inner city road tunnel. On one side it connects directly to a further tunnel system, which means that you can drive beneath the city centre for a distance of 8.5 kilometres.

Several mayors were forced to explain the problems involved in the construction of this time-consuming major project. When the earth subsided in 2008 in Stromovka Park, creating a huge crater 20 metres wide and 15 metres deep, Mayor Pavel Bém's opinion was that "things like that can happen." But another "thing like that" happened again five months later in the same place, and once more, not far away, in 2010. It was a miracle that no one was injured. Mayor Tomáš Hudeček, after examining the contracts concluded by his predecessor, declared the tunnel to be an unapproved project, bringing the work to a standstill. When further complications arose, his successor Adriana Krnáčová said that the structure must have been conceived by a "complete idiot." Whatever: the tunnel was opened four years later than planned, and the total cost rose to no less than 43 billion Kč.

Since 1989 the Czech language has had a new word: *tunelovat* – "to tunnel." This refers to the shady financial deals by which companies were financially hollowed out from within after the collapse of communism. In Prague's bar rooms it has long been suspected that Blanka is the perfect "tunnel" – in the new sense of the word. An analysis by an international legal firm concluded that Blanka was a collusion *par excellence* of politics and business. Which is why, shortly before the tunnel was inaugurated in 2015, the principal construction company put up posters across Prague with the slogan *Blanka is not a tunnel!*

Address Blanka tunnel complex, Prague, www.tunelblanka.info | **Getting there** By car via the Malovanka or Pelc-Tyrolka intersection, then straight ahead underground | **Tip** If that's not enough large-scale traffic construction for you, at the north entrance to the Blanka Tunnel note the new bridge over the Vltava in Troja.

12 ___ Bohemian Villages

Romantic relics from a bygone age

Like many other major European cities, Prague developed rapidly after the beginning of the industrial revolution. Although most of the surrounding villages were very quickly incorporated, their original village character has remained in several places beyond the city centre – though usually only in a few streets with an unmistakeable atmosphere.

Perhaps the most attractive example is to be found in the houses around the street Na Kocourkách in Střešovice. These are thought to date from the golden era of the Strahov Monastery, at the end of the 18th and beginning of the 19th century. The monks allocated plots of land to their employees on the sandstone rocks, to which some of the houses are literally clinging. Take a selfie on the park bench: everyone will think you're enjoying a holiday by the sea. Originally this area was much larger, but many of the houses have unfortunately been replaced by new ones. Take a short walk through the picturesque alleys Na Zástřelu and K Bateriím, and try not to look at the three concrete residential tower blocks in Ve Střešovičkách.

A little further on you'll find the picturesque remnants of what was once another village. Go into Staré Střešovice, then the street Pod Andělkou, right into Sibeliova and left into Nad Hradním Vodojemem. Although the architecture is less harmonious, and the new buildings spoil the scene, you cannot fail to notice the contrast between the former poor district and the magnificent villas beyond the rail tracks. The entrance to the famous Functionalist Villa Müller is in this street.

From the Baterie tram stop, any tram will take you to Vozovna Střešovice, where you can change to Tram 22 or 25 and continue to Drinopol. In the streets Za Strahovem and Nad Tejnkou you will find a less well-known, but equally romantic "village in the city."

Address Starting points: Na Kocourkách and Nad Tejnkou, 169 00 Prague 6, continue as directed in the text | **Getting there** Metro A to Hradčanská, then bus 184 to Kajetánka, up the hill on the streets Radimova, Na Zástřelu and Ve Střešovičkách | **Tip** If you travel from Břevnov to the city centre, get out at the Marjánka stop. The Moje Kredenc café at Bělohorská 26 is likely to be full, and you'll understand why if you have a coffee and cake there.

13 Bridge of the Intelligentsia
The tale of a track across the fields

Imagine you're walking on a track across fields next to railway lines that run relatively close to the city centre, and at a height of 19 metres. And if your imagination extends to a fondness for the walls of down-at-heel industrial buildings, an image of the Branický Bridge is taking shape in your mind's eye. The story of why the bridge is popularly known by a different name is best told as a fairy tale.

Once upon a time, there lived some people who weren't at all happy about freight trains thundering past their windows. So in the 1920s they decided to divert the rail tracks. But because people were thrifty in those times, in the end the diversion wasn't built. After a few years, other people came to rule the land – the communists. They were not so thrifty – on the contrary, they were very excited about establishing socialism. They decided to build the diversion after all, and started off with the biggest bridge. Doctors, professors and lawyers who had fallen under suspicion because they were not bursting with enthusiasm for establishing socialism were set to work there. Soon the structure was given the name "The Bridge of the Intelligentsia." In 1955 the workers completed construction and put two rail tracks on the bridge. The train lines just lay there. Nothing and nobody travelled along them, as the tunnel in the hill through which the trains would reach the bridge had yet to be dug. This took a further ten years. When the communists started to dig the tunnel, they noticed that the rock wasn't firm enough, and would fall on their heads if they made the tunnel too wide. That is why they only put one track through it. The second track on the bridge was thus superfluous, so they ripped it up again.

And they all lived happily ever after, as to this very day the trains cross the bridge on the single track, and we can take a pleasant walk alongside it.

Address Branický most, 147 00 Prague 4 | **Getting there** Tram 2, 3, 17, 21 to Nádraží Braník, then take the underpass to the bus station, walk a little way along Pikovická to the bridge and climb up to it via the steps by the bridge pier; on the other side of the bridge walk to the Malá Chuchle bus stop on Strakonická, where there is a connection to Smíchovské nádraží | **Tip** If you need to recover from the industrial decadence, get on your bike or put on your rollerblades, as one of Prague's most attractive bike paths leads directly under the bridge.

14 The Cable Car
Emulating James Bond

Do you love old James Bond films? If so, we have a secret to share with you. The fascination exerted by those classic movies is not only about Sean Connery's charm, the sexy Bond girls and the apocalyptically evil villains, but also about technology that seemed futuristic when the films were made, but nowadays just raises a smile. If you would like to play the role of Bond, a trip on the cable car of the NH Prague City hotel in Smíchov is a must: it has a striking similarity to the one that features in the closing scenes of *You Only Live Twice*.

In fact this cable car was constructed in 1996, and is the third and newest of its kind in Prague. Its purpose is to connect the lower and the upper parts of the hotel. Otherwise guests have to climb and descend 51 metres, or drive the long way round, three kilometres by car. The cable car takes only a minute, while providing an unusual view of Prague. In technical terms it is a funicular. It passes above the park path with the help of a sort of bridge. The journey costs nothing and you can use the cable car around the clock, which is apparently what many residents of Prague do if they live close to the upper hotel building. The entrance is slightly concealed: at the lower and upper reception you have to go a little to the left and look out for a metal door that looks like a normal lift entrance. You call the cable car just as you would summon a lift. It doesn't operate to a timetable – simply press the button, and it will arrive in no time at all, like a helpful genie out of the movies.

If you prefer not to go back down by the same route, you can walk through the park instead and take a look at the funicular from the outside. Or take a walk down the romantic and neglected street named U Mrázovky. It will lead you to the door of Villa Bertramka. This is where Mozart composed his great opera *Don Giovanni*.

Address Mozartova 261/1, 150 00 Prague 5, www.nhprague.com | **Getting there** Metro B, or tram 4, 5, 7, 9, 10, 12, 15, 16, 20, 21 to Anděl, then follow Plzeňská towards the flyover. The hotel lies beyond it on the left | **Tip** If you walk towards Anděl from the lower cable car station, then along Na Zatlance and U Nikolajky, you reach the small park called Na Skalce. This green oasis has a small pond with a waterfall and a romantic cast-iron shelter.

15 The Café in the Mill

A political hotspot on Kampa Island

President Miloš Zeman likes to mock his opponents as the "Prague coffee house." They in turn accuse him of declaring everyone with a different opinion to be a lazy Bohemian. Zeman is not referring to a vague opposition group, but in fact to a specific café that has been a thorn in his flesh for a long time: Mlýnská kavárna on Kampa, an island in the Vltava.

And no wonder: by day it's a family café, but in the evening it turns into a political zone, the unofficial camp of the supporters of Karel Schwarzenberg, whom Zeman defeated only narrowly in the presidential elections of 2013. While the president is sympathetic to Russia, it's here that the support for an American military base in the Czech Republic originated. Even ex-Secretary of State Condoleezza Rice was here. There's no shortage of well-known faces; the eccentric artist David Černý, for example, designed the bar counter.

The café can easily be recognised by its mill wheel, turned by an arm of the Vltava known as the Devil's Stream. The wheel provides the name of the café, often also known to regulars as "Mlejn" or "Kotas' place." The co-owner Martin Kotas is the life and soul of the café and of the above-mentioned initiatives. He's pleased to hear praise for his coffee, supplied by the bean roaster Mama Coffee; to go with the beer he serves Hermelin cheese in brine, made by hand in a workshop for the disabled close to Prague. This soft cheese is a must in every pub, and is also a good accompaniment for wine.

Those who leave after 10pm are asked by an elderly gentleman on the little wooden walkway that leads to the café to go quietly without talking. During the day he is an orchestra assistant at the Academy of Music; in the evening he ensures that the brother of the former Czech ambassador to the USA, who is joint owner of the building and lives above the café, gets a good night's sleep.

Address Všehrdova 449/14 (entrance via Kampa Park), 118 00 Prague 1, +420/257313222 | **Getting there** Tram 9, 12, 15, 20, 22 to Újezd, then walk to Kampa. The café is on the left after approximately 80 metres | **Hours** Daily noon–midnight | **Tip** The food in the café consists mainly of snacks to accompany beer and wine. For a filling meal, go to the excellent Uzbek restaurant Samarkand, at the first point you reach on Kampa Island.

16__The Cemetery
Horror in Bohnice

If you're in luck, the small metal gate next to the main entrance will creak open and let you in. You will then find yourself on a broad path that passes through the strangest cemetery in Prague, if not in the whole of the Czech Republic.

Cemeteries are usually sad places, but people often like to go there – perhaps for the tranquillity, perhaps for the many unknown persons who have passed away, at peace with their nearest and dearest, reconciled to death. But burials of that kind are a rarity in this cemetery: in most of the graves lie inmates of the psychiatric institute for which it was laid out in 1906. The exclusion of the mentally ill from society and inhumane methods of treatment make it unlikely that their lives came to a happy end. The same applies to the patients buried here who came from an institution in Trento, and were taken to safety when the front advanced in World War I. They died from typhus – like most of the soldiers who were brought to the hospital here.

A monument was erected to both of these groups, but only a few remains of the military memorial have survived. The bare stone column without an inscription and with a damaged cross emphasises the neglect of the cemetery since its closure in 1951 – although in recent years volunteers and the psychiatric institute itself have looked after it.

The ubiquitous ivy has swallowed up the last remaining gravestones. The sight of subsiding tombs and the burnt-out chapel are enough to send a shiver down your spine. This is an extremely creepy place. According to fans of inexplicable phenomena, the concentration of negative energy is unusually high here. Journalists' technical equipment is said to stop working here. Some people feel a burning in the soles of their feet, or attacks of cold. If you are immune to such sensations, we recommend visiting the cemetery in autumn. At twilight.

Address U Drahaně, 181 00 Prague 8 | **Getting there** Metro C to Kobylisy, then bus 102 to Staré Bohnice, go downhill along Bohnická, right into U Drahaně, left at the Bohnická farma therapy centre, and continue to the end, past allotments and fields | **Hours** Officially closed (enter at your own risk) | **Tip** From U Drahaně you can usually enter the grounds of the psychiatric institute (take the main entrance from Ústavní). You can use the Café V. kolona, where patients work as part of their therapy.

17 The Children's Cemetery

Traces of monstrous crimes

In the north-east corner of the cemetery in Ďáblice there is an expanse of grass beneath tall trees. Although at first sight it looks peaceful, this place is permeated with cruelty, and with grief which is hard to reconcile: the rows of graves are those of 43 children whose mothers were interned in communist camps in the 1950s. In a criminal episode that remains very little-known, the children died of hunger and thirst, in some cases because the camp guards took them from their mothers and left them to die without help. Their little bodies were secretly placed in deep shafts, the coffins piled one on top of the other. This was also the last resting place for adult inmates and human remains from the institute of pathology.

It was not until 1968 that some incomplete information about the existence of these mass graves emerged. The truth was known to a few families to whom the secret police had shown some mercy when they searched for their relatives. They were strictly forbidden to mark the graves, and the shafts were deliberately filled up with rubbish from the cemetery.

Only after 1989 did the Confederation of Political Prisoners succeed in finding at least some of the names of the buried persons in the archives, and establishing a memorial grave for them. In addition to the children's cemetery, this site holds the gravestones of 207 opponents of communism – including the priest Josef Toufar, who was tortured to death. A monument at the back of the cemetery commemorates resistance fighters killed by the Nazis. The shafts were used until 1943, and are the burial place of the paratroops who carried out the attack on Deputy Reich-Protector Reinhard Heydrich.

Despite occasional commemoration ceremonies, the cemetery is almost unknown – which doesn't alter the fact that few other places reveal the monstrous nature of communism in such a pure form.

Address Ďáblický hřbitov – north entrance, Ďáblická, 182 00 Prague 8 | **Getting there** Metro C to Ládví, then bus 103, 368 to Ďáblický hřbitov | **Hours** Jan – Feb, Nov – Dec 8am – 5pm; Mar – Apr & Oct 8am – 6pm; May – Sept 8am – 7pm | **Tip** From Ládví metro station, bus 166 takes you to the old rifle range at Prague-Kobylis (Kobyliská střelnice), a place of execution in World War II. After the attack on Reinhard Heydrich, the Nazis shot hundreds of people here, including the writer Vladislav Vančura, General Alois Eliáš and some residents of Lidice.

18   Chlebíčky

An essential delicacy

If you're walking through Prague and suddenly feel hungry, but only want a snack to take away, then there can only be one solution: head for the nearest *lahůdky* – delicatessen – and ask for *chlebíčky* – pronounced "klebitchki." Most of them will be visible behind glass under the counter. These are open sandwiches – of the very finest!

They may sound banal, but a delicious treat awaits you. On slices of white bread and butter, cut diagonally, the Czechs place anything that takes their fancy. This means miniature works of art with salami, cheese, caviar and boiled eggs; or ham, meat salad, gherkins and pickled paprika, salmon mousse and smoked fish – plus, an important ingredient, mayonnaise. They look good and they satisfy your appetite. A *chlebíček* is part of the country's daily bread, but also an essential element at every party.

A good place to start off your *chlebíčky* tour is the delicatessen Zlatý kříž at Jungmannova 34. The choice is enormous, the sandwiches are large by Czech standards, and the prices are unbeatable for this location. After that, take the Metro to Apetit, a patisserie whose address is Revoluční 12, close to Náměstí Republiky. Here, in a charming coffee house ambience, the cakes and other sweet snacks are complemented by a choice assortment of *chlebíčky*. Your next stop could be the small but elegant Libeřské lahůdky at Dukelských hrdinů 33. And from there, a journey of only one stop by tram takes you to the equally famous Chlebíčky Letná at Milady Horákové 42.

The origins of *chlebíčky*, by the way, came from a painter's easel in the interwar years: Jan Skramlík, who produced a portrait of the family of the famous delicatessen owner Jan Paukert, was unhappy that he constantly had to interrupt his work to satisfy his hunger with the little tit-bits that were usual at the time – a throwback to the Earl of Sandwich…

Address Zlatý kříž, Jungmannova 34, 110 00 Prague 1; see text for further addresses |
Getting there Zlatý kříž: Metro A, B to Můstek; Apetit: Metro B to Dlouhá třída; Libeřské
lahůdky: Tram 6, 8, 26 to Strossmayerovo náměstí; Chlebíčky Letná: Tram 1, 8, 12, 25, 26 to
Kamenická | **Hours** Zlatý kříž: Mon–Fri 6.30am–7pm, Sat 9am–3pm; Cukrárna Apetit:
Mon–Fri 7am–8pm, Sat & Sun 10am–8pm; Libeřské lahůdky: Mon–Fri 7am–7pm, Sat
& Sun 8am–6pm; Chlebíčky Letná: Mon–Fri 7.30am–7pm, Sat 8am–2pm | **Tip** If you'd
like to experiment by trying unconventional ingredients such as beetroot, horseradish or
herring on your *chlebíček*, Bistro Sisters at Dlouhá 39 is the place to go.

19 __ The Corrupt Tour
The best of the worst

When the philosopher and dramatist Petr Šourek proudly presented his new tour company Corrupt Tour at Prague's Holiday World trade fair in 2002, everyone asked the same questions: is this satirical? Or an anti-corruption campaign with a serious purpose? Or just a promising business start-up? The answer has to be: it's all of those things. It certainly is something special – and the Corrupt Tour has even made it on to the front page of the Wall Street Journal. The guides take you on a sightseeing tour of corruption, to places associated with lobbyists, over-priced contracts and the millions that have disappeared from the coffers of the Czech state. In short, there's never a dull moment!

Corrupt Tour is a normal travel company that sells tours as well as its own souvenirs, hires buses and employs its own guides, most of them actors. Their explanations of corruption are not only easier to understand than most newspaper articles, but are also spiced with absurd humour that alleviates for a brief moment the pain of hearing about the loss of taxpayers' money. On the Corrupt Tour you visit the "hawks' nests," i.e. the houses of leading Czech "godfathers" and lobbyists. It's only when you look at their luxurious residences, protected by walls and cameras, that you realise what kind of sums are involved in the corruption scandals. You get a glimpse inside hospitals that have become notorious for purchasing equipment at exorbitant prices. You hear the story of the Škodův palác, which the city government of Prague still rents on extremely unfavourable terms, and the history of the costly Blanka Tunnel, as well as the Prague transport authority and its financial shenanigans.

As the owner of the company remarks, when it comes to corruption, Prague has a lot to offer. And at the end of the tour you'll surely agree with him that you've seen the best of the worst.

Address Tours in Czech and English, starting at different places in the centre of Prague. Reservations: www.corrupttour.com | **Tip** The expression *zajít do cukrárny*, meaning "to go to the café," is part of the jargon of the people who pull the strings in the city. The office of the best-known lobbyist is above the Myšák café at Vodičkova 31, Prague 1. This restored historic patisserie became famous for its sweet dishes in the 1920s, for example the cake for the 80th birthday of President Tomáš Garrigue Masaryk.

20＿The Cubist Houses

Geometric visions at the foot of the Vyšehrad

In around 1910 a few Czech artists decided to apply Picasso's principles of clear edges, crystalline structures and interpenetrating planes to the field of architecture. This was the birth of something that only exists in the Czech Republic: architectural Cubism. Nowhere in the world are there as many Cubist buildings as in Prague. So it would be a pity to visit solely the House of the Black Madonna in Celetná.

On the banks of the Vltava, at the foot of the Vyšehrad rock, there are some works in this unique style that are perhaps even more striking. Following the redevelopment of the late 19th and early 20th century, which blighted areas including this district of raftsmen and timber dealers, new houses were built here. Josef Chochol, an impetuous, allegedly slightly neurotic architect who adhered almost slavishly to Cubist principles, managed to gain several commissions – for example, the white, three-storey villa that a builder called Bedřich Kovařovic constructed according to Chochol's designs. This villa stands within a geometric garden, and has an imposing monumental façade overlooking the Vltava. If you walk alongside the Cubist-style fence you get the impression that the projecting façade is turning to watch you. The best view of the villa is to be had from the railway bridge opposite.

Only a short distance away at the Rašín embankment, numbers 6–10, lies Chochol's red and white home for three families, with its mansard roof. But to see his most eye-catching work, go to the corner of Neklanova and Přemyslova. The apartment building that Chochol designed for his client František Hodek sticks out like the bows of a ship; unfortunately, ugly advertising signs now spoil its beautiful Cubist entrance.

Today these buildings are in private or commercial use, but just to look at them from the outside is to take a trip back to a great epoch.

Address Start: Villa Kovařovic, Libušina 3, 128 00 Prague 2, and continue as described | **Getting there** Tram 2, 3, 7, 17 to Výtoň | **Tip** Whereas the owners of the Cubist houses look after them, there is a nearby sight which is a monument to disgrace. The beautiful Art Nouveau station of Vyšehrad (Svobodova 2) is visibly decaying, and plans to restore it exist only on paper.

21 The Dairy

Changing prospects

In Riegrovy sady there is a small building, a protected monument from which there was once a view of the castle. At the end of the 20th century the prospects for this classical building were not rosy: 40 years of decay had taken their toll and necessitated the reconstruction of the building, which was in the middle of a park. As it was far from a water supply, drains or power lines, it seemed to the authorities to be such an expensive project that demolition was considered. Even when Jakub Vakoč approached the city government, no concessions were made to him. Every monument has a right to be torn down, it was said.

Following endless negotiations and later expensive reconstruction, as faithful as possible to the original building of 1830, the cosy restaurant called Mlíkárna – meaning "dairy" – now stands, thanks to Vakoč. The name is traditional. From 1902 there was a patisserie in the building. And because in those days cows still grazed in Riegrovy sady and the café sold their milk, it got its nickname.

Today's customers can still drink milk in their coffee here, beneath the same beautiful ceiling. The balustrade that flanks the outside steps and leads up to the two terraces is a well-made replica. The same applies to the façade in tree-bark style. This was the biggest challenge: it's no longer fashionable, and the façade simply refused to look like the original, although the masons did their best. In the end, the pattern was impressed in the plaster using sticks of wood. In summer you can drink your beer here in the shade of trees, and you don't even have to take several dogs along with you, as most of the regulars do.

Jakub Vakoč has leased the Dairy from the city government for 40 years. Today, prospects are good for the café. Only the tall trees now block the view of the castle. All the same, you will have a very pleasant time here.

Address Mlíkárna, Riegrovy sady, 120 00 Prague 2, www.facebook.com/Mlikarna | **Getting there** Tram 11, 13 to Vinohradská tržnice, then go along Budečská to Riegrovy sady park, or metro B, C to Florenc, and then bus 135 to Na Smetance | **Hours** Daily 11am–11pm | **Tip** If there's no space for you in the Dairy, walk a little further and have a beer in the Zahrádky Park Café, which is less cosy but has a big beer garden.

22   Dlouhá Gourmet Arcade

The artist is listening!

It was one of the last unredeveloped arcades that remained in the city centre. Today the passage between the streets named Dlouhá and Haštalská is dedicated to everyone who appreciates high-quality cooking, fresh ingredients and creative ideas.

At Bistro Sisters, for example, you can sample sandwiches prepared *à la tcheque*, in My Raw Café they stock exquisite cheeses, and in Via Del Vino choice Italian wines are sold. At the butcher's Naše maso, not only can you buy meat, but also have a freshly cooked steak prepared on the spot. The dinner served here is extremely popular: there is seating for only seven customers, and the waiting list is long.

The arcade was the concept of the wife of the Italian house owner, and she was also responsible for another feature: right under the ceiling, there are 3-D letters forming sentences such as "Yes, we're going right through to the back," or "You only have one child, don't you? That's enough." Translations are not provided, but perhaps locals will help you to understand the texts – out of gratitude because you've drawn their attention to this permanent installation, by the Czech artist Roman Týc.

This work can be interpreted as the immortalisation of the banal, or as a celebration of everyday life, but the artist himself offers a different explanation. Týc was reminded so strongly of the communist era by the shabby arcade that he thought about how secret agents must listen to a lot of banalities while spying on enemies of the state. As he believes this surveillance is still a topical subject, he carried out a three-month eavesdropping mission in the arcade. The lettering in the Dlouhá gourmet arcade reproduces scraps of conversation that Týc heard from passers-by. Even the words of the famous local butcher were carved in stone here. To give you a hint: it has something to do with aircraft.

Address Dlouhá 39, 110 00 Prague 1, www.gurmetpasazdlouha.eu | **Getting there** Tram 6, 8, 15, 26 to Dlouhá třída | **Hours** The arcade is open round the clock, and the shops have varying opening times. | **Tip** If you're still hungry after your visit, at Dlouhá 33 you will find the tavern Lokál, which serves excellent beer and down-to-earth Bohemian food, carefully prepared from selected ingredients.

23 The Educational Trail

Nine kilometres of contrasts

The residents of other districts don't associate anything especially beautiful with the names Vysočany, Prosek and Střížkov. Vysočany puts them in mind of industrial buildings, Prosek of ugly communist estates, and Střížkov probably only of the local football club, which seeks to rival the famous Bohemians Praha 1905.

What a pity! In reality all three districts are much more diverse, and these contrasts make the nine-kilometre educational trail highly interesting. You don't have to view its 21 stations and information panels in their entirety, or in sequence.

A good place to begin is Střížkov metro station. Said to be Prague's best-looking metro station, it has a futuristic design that resembles the skeleton of a whale. You might almost think you were in the middle of La Défense in Paris, if only the unending, depressing rows of concrete housing blocks of Prosek weren't there – you have to imagine the scene without them. In between lies pretty Friendship Park with its ponds and water channels.

A little further on, the path leads to the green of old Prosek, and you'd feel you were in a picturesque village if you hadn't just passed through one of the most colossal estates. From here you descend steeply and might need to muster a little courage, because the underpass leading to Vysočany station lies ahead. The entrance has been sprayed over with graffiti and the educational trail sign is overgrown. Still, it's definitely worth walking through the underpass – for a surprise!

The highlight of the Vysočany section is the beautifully restored Park Podvinní, with its Celtic fort in the shape of a lizard, plus a viewing platform, a tunnel and the Dragon Lake. From here, passing the bobcar track, the Prosek rock and houses, you reach the Teplická road – which reminds you why people in Prague have such a negative view of Prosek, Vysočany and Střížkov.

Getting there Naučná stezka, metro C to Střížkov, then follow the signs for the educational trail (a white square with a diagonal green stripe). Its website is www.mapy.cz: use the search term "Střížkov metro" then click "Změnit mapu" on the top left, then "Turistická." The dotted green line marks the trail "NS MČ Praha 9-SZ stezka." | **Tip** Information panel no.13 is named after a major Czech opera singer, Ema Destinnová. To see this unusual view of Prague you have to retrace your steps a little and take an almost invisible path that leads into the bushes at the corner of Nad Kundratkou and Na Stráži.

24 The Emmaus Monastery

Towers rebuilt from ruins

When the sirens wailed on 14 February, 1945, most people in Prague thought it was a false alarm. But shortly afterwards, 62 American planes opened their bomb bays. Their commander thought he was above the target of his attack – Dresden. The reason for this was that it was a very foggy day, and the radar wasn't working. This tragic mistake cost 701 human lives and destroyed dozens of buildings, including the Emmaus Monastery, which Charles IV founded in 1347 for Slav Benedictines. The bombs hit the vaulting, and completely destroyed the roof and towers of the monastery church.

Not until 1964 was a competition held for reconstructing the roof and towers. The architects were confronted with the question of what style they should adopt. The Gothic church had not been given its towers until the 17th century, when it was rebuilt in the Baroque style. In the 19th century its new occupants, Benedictines who had been driven out of Beuron in southern Germany, remodelled the exterior in the Gothic Revival style. They decorated the interior with frescoes in the so-called Beuron Style, which derived its colours, motifs and geometric shapes from Egyptian art and was later a source of inspiration for Art Nouveau.

The competition winner found an elegant solution to the style question by giving the church roof a completely new and modern form. He replaced the towers with enormous concrete wings, using more than a kilo of gold for the gilding of their tips. At a time when hardly any world-class art was being created in Czechoslovakia, this structure was praised by the international press, and today it remains a landmark of the New Town of Prague. Some see it as a ship's sail, others as rockets. Yet others regard it as the dark setting for a scene from Tolkien's *Lord of the Rings*, which is perhaps the most fitting commemoration of the unfortunate bombing attack on Prague.

Address Benediktinské opatství Panny Marie a sv. Jeronýma v Emauzích, Vyšehradská 49/320, 128 00 Prague 2, www.emauzy.cz | **Getting there** Metro B to Karlovo náměstí, or tram 2, 3, 4, 10, 14, 16, 18, 24 to Moráň or Karlovo náměstí | **Hours** May–Sept, Mon–Sat 11am–5pm; Apr & Oct, Mon–Fri 11am–5pm; Nov–Mar, Mon–Fri 11am–2pm | **Tip** The Prague 2 district, i.e. the New Town, was built by Charles IV to an exact urban plan, incorporating religious mysticism: if you join up the five churches on the city plan, they form a cross. The churches of St Catharine and Zvěstování Panny Marie Na slupi lie on the north–south axis, the churches of St Charles and the Emmaus Monastery on the east–west line. The centre of the cross is St Apollinaris.

25 Expo 58

The comrades' dream

This circular building rises proudly above the city, yet few people know the way to what used to be the Expo 58 Restaurant. What a shame! Although you can neither eat steak nor drink a cup of coffee here, and probably will not even be allowed inside, the harmonious architectural forms are still eye-catching.

In 1960 the building was brought from Brussels to Prague. In 1958 it stood on the site of the Brussels Expo world fair and, together with the exhibition pavilion, represented Czechoslovakia. The country's contribution to the Brussels Expo caused a sensation at the time and was given its highest award, the Golden Star. The jury enthused about the structure, which could be disassembled, and consisted of an iron framework, glass walls and elements made from plastic and other materials.

Unfortunately, the building no longer survives in its entirety. But at least the former restaurant can still be admired, looking as if it had been assembled from enormous parts of a child's building-block set. It's incredible that this structure, marked by the spirit of Functionalism, was constructed in a period when Socialist Realism was rampant. The reason was probably that the party comrades attached no great importance to the exhibition, so the architects were give a free hand. The theme of the pavilion was "A Day in Czechoslovakia," but as the failed communist economy was not capable of putting the items exhibited on the market, the idea was utopian.

It is certainly ironic that what used to be the Expo restaurant is now occupied by an advertising agency in the business of selling dreams. Its employees work in the space that was once the restaurant kitchen. However, the glass roof has had to be covered with blinds, supposedly because competitors were looking through it to take photographs and copy the ideas of the copywriters and graphic artists.

Address Restaurace Expo 58, Letenské sady 1500, 170 00 Prague 7 | **Getting there** Tram 6, 8, 17, 26 to Nábřeží Kapitána Jaroše, then follow the path up to Letenské sady | **Tip** Few exhibits remain from the Czechoslovakian display at the Expo, and the pavilion itself burned down in 1991. However, the aesthetics of this time can be viewed in the shape of a glass fountain, which was given a diploma of honour in Brussels, on the third floor of the National Technical Museum.

26 The Ferries

The romance of public transport

A Czech proverb says that you have the best view of the world when you're on horseback. In Prague, horses have competitors in the shape of the countless boats on the Vltava – with a view included.

The seven ferries are an alternative to the tourist ships. Admittedly they have no catering on board, and the crossing takes a matter of minutes, but you can use them with an ordinary ticket: the ferries are part of the public transport system. They are privately operated – possibly the reason why, on sunny weekends at peak times, they don't keep to their schedule, but run to and fro without a break.

The level of comfort on the boats varies: on an old tub, you'll take your seat on a hard wooden bench, in a modern vessel, on an upholstered sofa. In terms of landscape, too, the crossings are diverse. From ferry lines 1 and 2 you have views of the rocky natural surroundings of the northern edge of the city, and after disembarking you can continue along the Vltava, on foot or by bike, far beyond the boundaries of the city. Ferry lines 3, 5 and 7 are more urban. The connection between Smíchov, Výtoň and the island of Císařská louka on line 5, in particular, provides picture-postcard views of Prague's Hradčany castle, Vyšehrad and the historic buildings on Rašín Quay. Another noteworthy crossing is the new line 7 between Holešovice and Karlín, from which you see the market halls in Holešovice and also the castle from unusual angles.

The composition of the passengers changes as the day passes: at weekends most are trippers and cyclists, while on weekdays commuters use the ferries in the early morning and late afternoon. The crossing may be a shortcut on their way to work, and some of them like to chat to the ferrymen. Unlike the tram drivers, the crew on the boats always ply the same route, and often have a friendly word with their regular passengers.

Hours Ferry lines 1 and 2 operate all year, lines 3, 5, 6, 7 Apr–Oct. For timetables and other information see website: www.ropid.cz/en/ferries | **Tip** Learn more about the history of the Vltava by visiting the Podskalí customs house (Rašínovo nábřeží 30). Apart from the exhibition about rafts and everything connected with transporting wood by river, the cosy interior in log-cabin style is worth seeing.

27 Fivechurch Square

…which doesn't really exist

You won't find this address on maps of the city any more. However, the old lettering on the wall, Pětikostelská ulice (Fivechurch Lane), beneath the sign for the street called Sněmovní, shows that the picturesque little square was once really called Pětikostelní náměstí meaning "Fivechurch Square." Although this was its official appellation only until 1891, and then again during World War II, the people of Prague still call it by this name.

In fact this is a case of linguistic confusion. For one thing, there were only ever three churches here. St Andrew's was destroyed during the Hussite Wars, while St Martin's and St Michael's were demolished in the early 18th century. In truth the name of the square has nothing to do with places of worship, but derives from a noble family, once owners of the house at number 170, whose name, Fünfkirchen, means "five churches."

Today this quiet place is a contrast to the noise of Malostranské náměstí, as it is enclosed by the rear wing of the parliament and other historic buildings. Benches stand in the shade of trees, and grass grows in the cracks between the cobblestones. The only thing to disturb your peace of mind is the monument to Milada Horáková, who was executed in 1950 after a monstrous show trial. The artist has depicted this courageous resistance fighter and regime critic as a lark sitting on the microphone of a speaker's lectern. During her trial Horáková defended herself to the last. A few sentences from her last letter, one of the most moving documents in Czech history, are set into the paving stones.

On the upper part of the square, at one side you have a rare view of the dome of St Nicholas, on the other of the Hradčany castle. If you walk towards the Hradčany, you arrive at the cul-de-sac called U Zlaté studně and the luxury restaurant of the same name, which has a breathtaking view of Prague.

Address Sněmovní, 110 00 Prague 1 | **Getting there** Tram 12, 15, 20, 22 to Malostranské náměstí | **Tip** To reach the main entrance to the British embassy at Thunovská 14 you have to walk through a narrow passage between buildings. Apart from cameras and police, it is overseen by a bronze bust of Winston Churchill, who looks so obstinate that it's easy to see why he got the nickname "bulldog."

28 The Freight Station

From Žižkov to nowhere

The site of the Žižkov freight station has been the subject of heated debate for many years. On one side are the property developers, for whom this unused land is a tempting investment. They are opposed by architects and societies interested in converting the largest remaining Functionalist building in the city into a centre for education and art.

For a time it seemed as if the developers would win and the building would be torn down. The Czech railways, the original owner, had already sold part of the site to investors who planned a residential and office complex. However, after the freight station was given the status of a protected monument in 2013, the prospects for saving it grew brighter. Moreover, in 2016 the government decided to move the home of the National Film Archive, bit by bit, to the freight yard office block. The archive now runs a small café here, and it has plans for a summer cinema and further cultural events. Part of the building is let to private companies, so the station is accessible to the public.

If you love the romance of industry, don't miss it. This complex of reinforced concrete began operating in 1936; the freight yards were mainly used by trains carrying foodstuffs, which were also stored here. The tracks, with a series of monumental iron elevator towers, run between two storehouses. The cellars of the stores, with ceilings several metres high and Functionalist columns, are also an impressive sight. At the end of the tracks stands the office building. From its terrace you can get a good view of the whole site.

Trucks collected and delivered goods from here until the end of the 20th century. Then operations came to a gradual halt. Discussions between developers, the city authorities and the current tenants are continuing, but how this once-majestic freight station will look in the future is an unanswered question.

Address Jana Želivského 2, 130 00 Prague 3, www.nadrazi.nfa.cz | **Getting there** Tram 9, 10, 11, 16, 26 to Nákladové nádraží Žižkov | **Hours** Dependent on the events programme, see website | **Tip** At Želivského metro station, take a look at the Dorint Don Giovanni Prague hotel (Vinohradská 157a). Then you might want to avert your eyes. With rare unanimity, both locals and architecture buffs alike regard it as one of the ugliest buildings in Prague. Its nickname is "the pink cake."

29   Garden Café Taussig

More than just a café…

There are many cafés in Prague where you can eat and drink in the open air, which is why many of them have a name that includes the word "garden." But the outdoor terrace of Garden Café Taussig is so spacious that it beats all the others in Prague hands down. Nevertheless, not many people know this place: at first glance it is easy to overlook the garden, though it covers an area of almost 8,000 square metres. From the main entrance you can only see a few tables, up on a broad concrete approach. However, if you walk up and then take a long flight of steps, adapted for the physically disabled with mobility handicaps, you come to a path on the right flanked by more places to sit. You have to carry your cup of coffee there yourself, because there's no waiter service, but the reward for this is a superb view of the castle. The path winds upwards, and when at last you reach the top – high up, wonderfully solitary – you will understand how special this café is.

The cascading appearance of the garden is a clue to the fact that it was once a vineyard. That was a long time ago, and the Taussig family no longer owns the adjoining building. It was once a kind of summerhouse for leisure and enjoyment, and only became a year-round residence in the early 19th century.

For decades the house has been a residential home for the mentally handicapped – and this is one more good reason to come here for coffee and cake. The café is a project that aims to integrate the residents who work there into society, by giving them more independence and confidence. A slogan on the sign outside, perhaps a little cryptic at first, draws attention to its social purpose: *Garden Café Taussig. A café that helps.* You might not expect to find heartwarming help of that kind here. The prices, which are extremely reasonable for such a location, also come as a welcome surprise.

Address Vlašská 25, 118 00 Prague 1, www.cafe-taussig.cz | **Getting there** Tram 12, 15, 20, 22 to Malostranské náměstí, then bus 192 to Nemocnice pod Petřínem, and up the streets Karmelitská, Tržiště and Vlašská | **Hours** May–Sept, Mon–Fri 11am–7pm, Sat & Sun noon–7pm | **Tip** A little way down in Vlašská, in front of the German embassy, you can see some stone buffers, relics of the days when horse-drawn carriages were the principal means of transport, and their parking spaces looked like this. The tops of the stones have been polished smooth by the hands of generations of children from Malá Strana who have used them for playing leapfrog.

30__ Garden in Šternberg Palace

Perfectly hidden on the castle square

You only need to take a few steps, and then the rustling of a colourful carpet of leaves overlays the noise of the city. Fish wriggle around the pond, closely observed by an elegant bronze stork. Other visitors speak in low voices so that they don't disturb the atmosphere. You might think you were in the garden of a country mansion, but in fact one of the places with the highest density of tourists in Prague, the castle square, is only a few metres away. Welcome to the garden of Šternberg Palace.

There must be more than one reason why so few people know about this enchanting spot. One of them is surely that Šternberg Palace is not visible from the castle square. The entrance is situated in the left-hand part of the archbishop's palace, and you have to pass through a narrow alley to reach Šternberg Palace. The National Gallery uses the halls of the palace to accommodate one of its permanent exhibitions, and few visitors think to explain at the ticket desk that they only want to spend some time in the garden, and will save the great works of El Greco, Rubens and Dürer for another time.

After their art-viewing marathon, palace visitors are often quite simply too tired to visit the garden. That is truly a pity, if only because interesting statues of Czech artists from the first half of the 20th century have been placed here. The entrance to the garden, by the way, is at the back of the courtyard on the left, in a corridor that leads to the toilets.

There's a café in the courtyard, furnished in a style that well matches the artistic character of the whole building, while the bar and what is on offer there seem a throwback to the 1980s. The particular charm of this spot owes something to the friendly waiters, who not only let you carry your coffee into the garden but are also willing lend you cushions when you get there.

Address Šternberský palác, Hradčanské náměstí 15, 118 00 Prague 1, www.ngprague.cz/objekt-detail/sternbersky-palac | **Getting there** Tram 22 to Pohořelec, then go in the direction of the castle | **Hours** Apr–Oct, Tue–Sun 10am–6pm (times approximate, depending on the weather) | **Tip** If you're not yet tired of greenery in the city, walk through Jelení příkop. One of the entrances is in the street U Brusnice, and you can walk along this little valley to the Malostranská metro station.

31 Havel's House

Where the president slept behind bars

Since 2013, all passengers flying into Prague have landed at Václav Havel Airport. But don't expect to find other buildings or streets named after the most significant Czech of the late 20th century – the city authorities seem to believe they've done enough renaming in the last 100 years, and the airport will have to suffice.

At least they considered naming the Rašín embankment between the Jirásek and Palacký bridges after Havel. Here, at number 78, the famous critic of the Czechoslovakian regime spent most of his life. It was built in 1905 by his grandfather, the owner of a building company who also constructed the Lucerna arts centre and left his signature – lots of plasterwork, loggias and tripartite windows – on the house on the Rašín embankment. This has been the address of the Havel family for more than 100 years.

Václav Havel himself occupied it until 2003, before moving into a villa in Dejvice. The Charter 77 petition was drawn up in his third-floor apartment; the address is given in the document's contact details. The telescopes of the secret police were trained on the building from a permanent observation post in the nearby water tower. The foundation of the Civic Forum was decided on here in 1989.

Havel and his architect friend Vlado Milunić also dreamed of a project with Frank Gehry, and since 1996 Gehry's Dancing House has stood next door. Milunić, neighbour of the future president, renovated Havel's apartment before the collapse of the communist regime. He divided the living room from the study with metal bars and placed a simple bed behind them – so that Havel, who was often imprisoned, would feel at home there.

With his characteristic sense of humour, Havel would perhaps have been pleased that the airport that now bears his name was formerly called Ruzyně – just like the prison that so often held a man who was afraid of flying.

Address Rašínovo nábřeží 2000/78, 120 00 Prague 2 | **Getting there** Tram 5, 17 or bus 176 to Jiráskovo náměstí | **Hours** Not open to the public | **Tip** Another place associated with Havel is the wine bar Na Rybárně in Gorazdova ulice, where many important meetings took place during the Velvet Revolution. It is now a Vietnamese bistro. The original fish decoration remains on the walls.

32 Havlíčkovy sady

Do you recognise the ideology?

When the German industrialist and man of taste Moritz Gröbe decided to settle in Prague in the 1870s, the place he chose was a sunny vineyard slope between Vinohrady and Vršovice. He landscaped the estate in the style of an English garden and built himself a luxury villa in Neo-Renaissance style. Then he was afflicted by bad luck. He was only able to hold his garden parties for three years before a stroke claimed his life. His heirs sold the property to the city government, which opened it to the public in 1906. Officially its name is Havlíčkovy sady, but to this day the people of Prague only ever call it Grébovka, after the founder.

For many years after the 1989 revolution it was a decaying, unwelcoming spot. However, the estate regained its old appearance when the park was restored. On the south-facing slope you can see the vineyard, which was known long ago to Charles IV, and an impressive wooden wine parlour where you can try the local vintages. Romantics, too, are catered for here: in the upper section of the park there is an artificial grotto with a fountain and a statue of Neptune. In Gröbe's lifetime what is now called Café Pavilon had a shooting gallery, chess tables, and a skittle alley that still exists: relaxation and recreation have always been the watchwords here.

The villa itself has been completely renovated. In World War II it was made over to the Hitler Youth, and after 1953 to the communist Young Pioneers. Today it's the home of an NGO that provides training to lawyers in countries that are undergoing transformation. Thus it reflects the history of the 20th century.

The house only opens for the traditional autumn grape harvest. Don't be surprised by the hammer and sickle above the marble stairs. This communist symbol was left here as part of the history of the site, even though it would have offended Moritz Gröbe's taste.

Address Havlíčkovy sady, 120 00 Prague 2 | **Getting there** Tram 4, 22 to Krymská, then walk. The entrance to the park is in Rybalkova ulice. | **Hours** Daily: Sept–Apr 6am–10pm, May–Aug 6am–midnight | **Tip** "Truth triumphs, but it's hard work." This quote and a bust of its author, the postwar foreign minister Jan Masaryk, is on the gate of the house at no. 22 in the street named after him. Masaryk was born in 1886 in Villa Osvěta.

33 The Historic Waterworks

A hidden-away museum

In Prague, getting drinking water is no problem at all. A more difficult business is answering the question of when the Museum of the Prague Water Supply in the waterworks at Podolí is open. This secret can be revealed on the website of the Prague Water and Sewerage Company by clicking on "Zážitková turistika" – which means "tourist experience."

Perhaps this is why not many citizens of Prague know the museum. Nevertheless, it's well worth visiting its monumental building, dating from the 1930s, and not just to admire the overwhelming architecture by Antonín Engels – who also, by the way, created the large, circular open space in Dejvice, the Kulaťák. In his day, Engel was no architectural prophet. Quite the reverse: his contemporaries accused him of mixing styles, for example in the Cubist windows of the neoclassical façade, behind which the Functionalist vault of the waterworks is concealed. Yet this vault above the filtration hall is one of the highlights of the museum. A further treasure is a section of water pipe from antiquity, which can be compared with a pipe dating from the age of Emperor Rudolf, allowing visitors to judge for themselves how little these things changed over the centuries. Among numerous other interesting items are a pump dating from 1830, photographs of the construction of water pipelines and a collection of water meters.

You will also find out when and why the Prague waterworks began to add chlorine, and why the plant at Podolí is only a back-up facility today. In the second part of the tour, which lasts almost one and a half hours, the remarkable process of purifying water is explained in detail, and visitors are taken up the water tower, from where they have a fantastic view of the city. Now at last you'll agree that classifying the waterworks as a "tourist experience" is, perhaps, not so strange after all.

Address Podolská vodárna, Podolská 15, 140 00 Prague 4 | Getting there Tram 2, 3, 17, 21 to Podolská vodárna. Podolská street is behind the waterworks. | Hours Tours: Thu 11am, 1pm, 3pm; tickets must be purchased at least four days in advance from www.ticketstream.cz; enter "Muzeum pražského vodárenství" in the search box | Tip Walk along the Vltava towards the city centre to the Podolka restaurant. You can enjoy its creative specialities – not all vegetarian – just by the river.

34 __ The Hotel International

The mad confectioner

This is a monumental example of Socialist Realism, a style of architecture and art that the Soviet Union exported to its satellite states, which is now viewed with scorn. To this day the hotel still shows what luxury looked like under the direction of communism.

The building with the five-pointed star on its roof was constructed between 1952 and 1956. Originally intended as military quarters, it later served to accommodate Soviet delegations, in comfort. Under the auspices of the notorious minister of defence Alexej Čepička, who fantasised that Stalin himself would attend the inauguration, the building in wedding-cake style took on such dimensions that it was nicknamed "the mad confectioner's dream." Stalin didn't live long enough to see it completed, and when it became clear that not so many Soviet delegations were making the journey to Czechoslovakia, the International became a luxury hotel for tourists from abroad.

When you enter the lobby, it seems at first sight to be a normal hotel. But take a closer look at details like the gilded door handles, the marble-clad columns and the lime tree leaves on the ceilings. Near the bar there hangs a yellowing tapestry depicting motifs of Prague: at its centre is the monument to Stalin on Letná hill, known to the people of Prague as "queuing for meat." It was blown up in 1962 after the end of the Stalin cult.

It's worth paying a visit to the VIP rooms on the 14th and 15th floors. If they're not open, ask at the reception desk if you can see them. The gigantic crystal chandelier and the flower mosaic by Max Švabinský on the staircase are also worth a look, as is the conservatory, from where you get a breathtaking panoramic view of Prague. All you have to do is imagine the Soviet generals sitting here with their vodka and caviar, and you're back in the old Czechoslovakia of communist cadres.

Address Koulova 15, 160 00 Prague 6, www.internationalprague.cz | Getting there Metro
A to Dejvická, then tram 8, 18 to Nádraží Podbaba | Hours Always open | Tip From the
hotel take bus 116 or 160 to Břetislavka and stroll along the picturesque road V Šáreckém
údolí past fine houses, mills and agricultural estates.

35 House Signs
Images of old Prague

Walking down Nerudova, the lane that is the last stage of the coronation route, is an essential part of the tourist programme. But pause for a moment. Raise your eyes above the windows of the souvenir shops and tourist traps and you'll discover the world of house signs.

These reliefs and statuettes gave the houses their names, and until the 18th century, when Empress Maria Theresa introduced house numbers, they provided orientation in the city. Some 200 house signs remain in Prague, the most attractive of them in Nerudova. They indicated the rank, profession or name of the owner, though the precise origin is known only of a few. One of these is the house known as The Three Fiddles, which was occupied by three families of violinists. It's said that a ghostly concert can be heard there at full moon. The house called The Golden Cup belonged to a goldsmith: the vessel was one of the oldest symbols of his guild. Gold was a popular attribute, as buildings with names such as The Golden Eagle and The Golden Key demonstrate. Some signs were three-dimensional, while others were small paintings, like the sign of The Golden Horseshoe, on which St Wenceslas is depicted on a horse shod in gold.

Animal motifs, like the red lamb or the green crab, were also common. A more unusual sign is the white swede. A rare symbol can be found on Morzin Palace, where two Moors support the balcony. They qualify as signs because they gave the building its name, The Moors.

A highlight of Nerudova is the famous house called The Two Suns. This was the home of Jan Neruda, author of the picturesque *Tales of the Little Quarter*. It's situated almost at the top of the road. If you're hungry for more, carry on into Úvoz, but if you already have a crick in your neck, turn right instead and climb up to the castle, where you have a wonderful panoramic view of Prague.

Address Nerudova, 118 00 Prague 1 | **Getting there** Tram 12, 15, 20, 22 to Malostranské náměstí, then go across the square and up into Nerudova | **Tip** In the 13th century Nerudova was divided in the middle by the castle walls built by Otakar II of the Přemysl dynasty. At the spot where the green house at no. 19 narrows the alley, the Strahov Gate stood until 1711. Watch out! Around midnight every Friday, a fiery carriage is said to pass through, carrying a skeleton seeking release from a curse.

36 The Hrabal Wall

Wild weddings, rough streets

At the corner of Ludmilina and Na Hrázi, a column proudly bearing the inscription *Foundation stone – Bohumil Hrabal Centre* rises from the ground. The fact that it has stood here, alone and neglected, since 2004, would surely have made the author laugh heartily, and led him to put the story into the mouth of his well-known character Uncle Pepin. Bohumil Hrabal lived in Libeň for more than 20 years, and he loved this seedy district. Although the locals are proud of their famous son, the memorials to him which do exist are not exactly fitting.

From 1950 to 1973 Hrabal lived in a small room at 326/24 Na Hrázi. Here his wild "weddings at home" were celebrated: from published banns, he would note the names of brides and bridegrooms, and although he didn't known the happy couple personally, he would party all night with friends in their honour. During the day he wrote his books on the roof of the backyard workshop. In 1988 the house went, to make way for the metro and the bus station. In 1999, two years after the author's death, this huge, empty concrete terminal was at least renamed Bohumil Hrabal Square.

The foundation stone of the Hrabal Centre, by the way, stands on land that a private company bought from the transport authority. Although the firm announced the construction of a multi-use building, nothing has happened here for years. It's not even certain that the Hrabal Centre will ever be built.

The most fitting memorial to the most-translated Czech author of the 20th century was painted in 1999 on the metro wall that forms most of the street Na Hrázi: Hrabal, larger than life, next to his typewriter, with a glass of beer, his cats and quotes from his works. It's sad to record that the site of this mural is an ugly car park – but who knows? Perhaps the novelist, with his liking for run-down places, would have approved for exactly that reason.

Address Na Hrázi, 180 00 Prague 8 | Getting there Metro B to Palmovka | Tip The carefully restored Libeň manor house seems like a survival from bygone days, and like the nearby park Thomayerovy sady it's well worth a visit.

37 Idiom

The physics of language

Library of Babel is the title of a story written by Jorge Luis Borges. It's a pity he didn't live to hear that this library actually now exists in Prague. In the lobby of the municipal library is an impressive tower of books which rises to a height of five metres: this is a work of art called *Idiom*.

The Slovak artist Matej Krén, who lives in Prague, used 8,000 books to make this colossal, colourful structure. Take a look inside the opening in its lower part.– the interior is breathtaking, as mirrors above and below multiply the view and create an infinite tower of books. Just make sure that you don't lean too far forward and spoil the optical illusion with your own reflection.

In 1994 this sculpture won the critics' award as well as the people's prize at the São Paulo Biennial, and a photo of the work appeared on the cover of *Science* magazine.

Back home in Prague, the work was permanently installed inside the city library in 1998.

Today the library holds more than 344,000 books, and the interior of *Idiom* demonstrates their wide range of genres, languages and authors. Avant-garde books, classics, rare and precious works, pulp fiction and thrillers are placed in direct proximity, as are the works of Czech and international authors, both famous and forgotten. From time to time, someone among the streams of visitors feels bold enough to test the laws of physics by trying to pull out a book. For this reason the library has to stabilise the sculpture every year, and replace books that have lost their structural soundness with new additions. This means that the work is constantly changing, reflecting changes in language and idiomatic nuances.

To give a free translation of the words of Borges: "There is no syllable one can speak that is not full of tenderness and terror, that is not, in one of these books, the name of a god."

Address Městská knihovna, Mariánské náměstí 1/98, 110 00 Prague 1, www.mlp.cz |
Getting there Metro A or tram 2, 17, 18 to Staroměstská | **Hours** Mon 1–8pm, Tue–Thu
9am–8pm, Sat 1–6pm | **Tip** If you're short of cash, go to the ground-floor cafeteria for the
cheapest snack around.

38 __ The Invalidovna

An endangered Baroque gem

The hospital for veteran soldiers is an imposing edifice that can certainly stand comparison with the French building on which it was based – although only one ninth of the project was completed. Today its long, empty corridors and vaulted ceilings are a magnet for film-makers: here F. Murray Abraham played his starring role as Salieri in Miloš Forman's *Amadeus*. The Invalidovna is rarely open to the public, but even from the outside this magnificent building evokes a special atmosphere.

Like the Hôtel des Invalides in Paris, the hospital in Karlín was intended to house war veterans. In 1737, seven years after construction began, work was suspended when the foundation responsible ran out of money. The plans, which originally envisaged 4,000 residents, were cut back. Nevertheless, the site was provided with workshops, a bakery and butcher's shop, a hospital, a chapel and a prison, in addition to accommodation for veterans. The building served its purpose until 1935, when the soldiers were moved to a new home. After the war it was occupied initially by the archive and stores of the National Technical Museum, then by a military archive. During the exceptional floods of 2002, the water was 3.2 metres deep here, and so much archive material was damaged that most was frozen to preserve it; restoration will be carried out when money is available.

Since 2013 the building has lain empty. The Charles University has expressed interest, but doesn't have the two billion Kč necessary to convert it into a campus. The state will probably sell it to a private investor, and it's feared that, as happens so often in Prague, the conditions stipulated by the conservation authorities will not be respected, and the Invalidovna might lose its unique character irretrievably. It's a great pity that entire buildings can't be frozen until better times come along.

Address Za Invalidovnou 3, 186 00 Prague 8 | **Getting there** Metro B or tram 3, 8, 24 to Invalidovna, then walk approximately 150 metres along Sokolovská in the direction of Kaizlovy sady | **Hours** Open to the public only on special occasions, including the Open House weekend (www.openhousepraha.cz/en) | **Tip** Only one other notable Baroque building remains in this whole district: the small chapel by the former military cemetery. It stands opposite Pernerova ulice 59.

39 _ The Jan Palach Memorial
Flames of steel

When in January 1969 Jan Palach doused his body in petrol and set himself alight, in protest against the occupation of Czechoslovakia, the increasing "normalisation" of society and the apathy of the Czech people, the square in front of the Philosophical Faculty was renamed "Náměstí Jana Palacha" by students. The regime, however, had no wish to preserve the memory of Palach's act, and it quickly reverted to Red Army Square. Only after the Velvet Revolution 20 years later was the open space between the Rudolfinum, the Philosophical Faculty and the Academy of Art officially named Jan Palach Square.

A further 25 years passed before a memorial to Palach was erected there. It was made in the studio of the artist John Quentin Hejduk, who gave visual expression to a poem by the American author David Shapiro that captured the atmosphere of Palach's funeral, and the immeasurable suffering of his mother. The giant sculptures, from which symbolic flames rise, are entitled *The Son's House* and *The Mother's House*, and were first exhibited in 1991 in Prague castle. On that occasion Hejduk, invited to Prague by President Václav Havel, donated the two works to the city, in the form of preliminary models in wood. The city government undertook the obligation of casting them in metal for public display, but this took many years. The inauguration did not take place until January 2016, 16 years after the death of Hejduk.

The two steel cubes stand in a corner of the square with the memorial plaque bearing Shapiro's poem. *The Mother's House*, made of weatherproof steel, is darker, seemingly rusty, and its flames seem to turn in on themselves in quiet desperation. The flames on the bright *Son's House*, made from stainless steel, create a bold contrast. They are directed symbolically to the castle, the centre of power that Jan Palach defied in 1969 through his courageous act.

Address Corner of Alšovo nábřeží and Náměstí Jana Palacha, 110 00 Prague 1 | **Getting there** Metro A to Staroměstská | **Tip** In the Philosophical Faculty building there is a copy in metal of the death mask made by the sculptor Olbram Zoubek at the Institute of Forensics, to which Palach's body had been taken. Zoubek went there with a former schoolmate, a burns specialist, and the porter defied the rules to let them in.

40 The Jeep Bar
A place to get tanked up

Imagine the scene: a quiet residential quarter, a little black garden gate – and a piece of artillery on the lawn. This treasured item stands proudly on the grass in front of the Jeep Bar. No actual jeeps are to be seen, but their spirit is omnipresent.

Above the main gate hangs the front radiator of a jeep – like a pair of bison antlers from one of the settlements founded by the Western-inspired "Czech Tramping" movement. Spare parts and numerous pictures of the famous vehicle, that some believe contributed to the American victory in World War II, cover the walls of the cellar, where guests can sit at the bar or one of three small tables. "Made in the USA" is an endorsement here, just as it is among the "tramps." Since 1993 the Stars and Stripes has waved from the tall flagpole, while beneath it in the beer garden draught beer is tapped from the keg and the drinkers sit around diesel drums instead of tables. It goes without saying that everything is decorated with military symbols – for example the wheelbarrow that bears the initials U.N.R.R.A., plus its dimensions and contents. The dominant feature of the scene, however, is the barbecue, a cut-away water-tank car – a star of the screen that appeared in Jan Svěrák's *Dark Blue World*. Other items here, such as the OT-810 tank, have also been seen in Czech films, though usually in the role of villains – on the side of the German army.

The owner of the Jeep Bar is passionate about military history, and interested in the weaponry hardware of all nations. The cannon in the garden is in fact a Soviet howitzer that once served as a memorial to the Red Army in Moravia. Unlike most such relics, it didn't end up in a museum or a scrap yard, and today, thanks to the tender loving care of the owner, its barrel proudly points to the sky in the district of Smíchov – while the guests around it get completely bombed.

Address Pod Lipkami 16, 150 00 Prague 5, www.jeepbar.cz | **Getting there** Metro B to Anděl, then tram 9, 10, 15, 16, 21 to Klamovka and up along the streets Podbělohorská and Pod Lipkami | **Hours** Mon–Fri 6pm–midnight | **Tip** In the same street, a small sign at no. 24 claims that it was the site of a quarry from which the foundation stone of the National Theatre was obtained. This is a little joke on the part of the owner of the garage on which the sign is placed. Historical records of the foundation of the sacred home of Czech drama say nothing about this supposed source.

41 Johannes Nepomuk
A sad statue

More than 200 years separate the late Baroque and Cubist styles, but in the street called Spálená they look good alongside each other. The gap in the buildings between the Church of the Trinity and the Diamant tenement is the location of a sight in which the two styles are combined in a most original way. Unfortunately it attracts little attention, as it has been in a poor condition for years. Yet there are several reasons for visiting it.

The statue of St John Nepomuk was made in the early 18th century along with the church, which was built by Christoph Dientzenhofer and others. Its creator is thought to have been Michal Jan Josef, from the Brokoff family of sculptors.

In the 20th century the church fell into ruin, and took on the role of a deserted place of worship in films, but it was later restored. However, the statues at the side – including, on the left, Judas Thaddeus, probably by Matthias Bernhard Braun – were forgotten.

The Cubist house next door was built 200 years later. Its architect, Emil Králíček, connected his building to its Baroque neighbour by erecting a Cubist canopy above the statue, an act that initially drew protests, though it's acknowledged today as a praiseworthy intervention.

Behind the figure of the saint, Králíček designed a small garden, with a brick well by the church wall and a gate with two Cubist columns. It can be reached from the cul-de-sac Magdalény Rettigové, but its charm has been lost. The garden has disappeared beneath paving, and one of the columns has given way to an ugly lift for the metro, while a container stands in front of the other – and the well is crumbling. The statue of the saint has been damaged: someone has stolen lead from the canopy, and the five stars that surround Nepomuk's head on other depictions of the saint are now hanging round his neck. That's not how stars should look.

Address Church of the Trinity: Spálená 6; Diamant: Lazarská 1, 110 00 Prague 1 |
Getting there Metro B to Národní třída, then go along Spálená | **Tip** Take a look inside
the Church of the Trinity to see how the Slovak Greek Catholics have made their church
family-friendly. During Mass, children can play in a specially made little house.

 Josef Sudek's Studio
Misted over, ice-covered, rain-spattered

Josef Sudek's studio will delight even those who've never heard of the renowned Czech photographer. It's situated in one of those charming back yards of Malá Strana that are not otherwise accessible to tourists: just press the doorbell next to the entrance to house numbers 28/30/32 in the street Na Újezdě.

The reason why no fewer than three numbers are next to the door becomes clear as soon as you walk through the passage and enter the little yard, where several doors lead to the apartments. One tenant even has his own private yard, but go straight on: beyond the metal gate and a further passage, a much larger, brighter courtyard awaits.

At the heart of the city, but still in a quiet location, lies one of the most original galleries in Prague. The artists who exhibit here are not well known, but are all the more interesting for that. Simply follow the notice on the wall: *Fotograf v zahradě*, which means "photographer in the garden," and you'll come to a wooden bungalow. This is where the one-armed master, who once captured on film the genius loci of St Vitus' Cathedral, the magical gardens of Střešovice and the woods of Beskyd, fished his prints out of the developing tray. Here you can look out of the window that the photographer recorded for years, its pane of glass like a camera's diaphragm between his inner world and the outside – sometimes misted over, sometimes ice-covered, sometimes spattered with rain.

The fact that this is a replica of the original building, which burned down in 1985, shouldn't concern you. That's why, apart from some items of furniture and an old stove, nothing remains of Sudek here, and why there's no museum either, though an exhibition is devoted to him every year. Rather, his presence is implicit. It's as if the motto about his craft also applied to his studio: "Photography shouldn't show everything, photography should suggest."

Address Újezd 30, 118 00 Prague 1, www.atelierjosefasudka.cz | Getting there Trams 12, 15, 20, 22 to Újezd, then 100 metres on foot; from the National Theatre, tram 9 to the Újezd stop round the corner in Vítězná | Hours Tue−Sun noon−6pm | Tip In the flat where Josef Sudek lived at Úvoz 24 is a gallery that displays his work and that of other artists.

43 Karel Zeman Museum

Who wants a leading role in an animated film?

Close to the Charles Bridge lies a gateway to the realm of fantasy: the Karel Zeman Museum. This film director, who numbers Steven Spielberg among his fans, created many fantasy and fairy-tale films. Although his animated movies are over 50 years old, they seem anything but old-fashioned.

The museum is like a film studio. Rooms filled with monitors, photographs and film sets are devoted to the works of Zeman, and familiarise visitors in a playful manner with the technology of his animations, dating from the period between 1950 and 1980. *Journey to the Beginning of Time*, for example, is the story of four boys who discover mammoths, dinosaurs and trilobites during a boat trip. The museum display not only explains prehistoric times, but also demonstrates how Zeman filmed the mammoth scenes. Try it out for yourself: sheets of paper arranged one behind the other in different ways suddenly turn into a 3-D image when they're viewed from the front, through the lens of a camera or a mobile phone.

Visitors can have interactive fun in the rooms dedicated to the film entitled An Invention for Destruction. If you go there with children, you'll never get them away from the flying machine. Thanks to the moving cinema screen behind the machine, it seems on the video footage as though you're flying through the air. Or join in the adventures of *The Fabulous Baron Münchhausen* and transport your image to the moon. If you so wish, to round things off you can put yourself into film scenes, using a camera and software.

The museum was established in 2012 by two fans of Zeman; they received help in setting it up from the daughter of the maestro, who made available detailed screenplays including sketches of settings, and other items from her father's archive. These treasures clearly illustrate Zeman's great love of the playful world of animated moving pictures.

Address Saská 3, 118 00 Prague 1, www.muzeumkarlazemana.cz | **Getting there** Tram 12, 15, 20, 22 to Malostranské náměstí, then walk along Mostecká | **Hours** Daily 10am–7pm, last admission 6pm | **Tip** For film fans: the late Baroque house at Hroznová 1, in a romantic site on the banks of the Čertovka, was the home of Jiří Trnka, a famous director of animated films.

44 Karlín

The quarter on the water

No quarter of Prague has experienced more radical change in the last quarter century than Karlín. Before the political transformation of 1989 it was a down-at-heel working-class district and the butt of jokes: "Libeň and Karlín – not places to be seen!." Today, however, shiny new buildings stand next to restored historic houses. The locals no longer spend their time in smoke-filled pubs, but in cafés, bistros, design shops and pretty parks.

Karlín was full of potential from its early days. The district was planned on the drawing board in 1817 to prevent the uncontrolled building of houses that, it was feared, would result from the inward migration of large number of factory workers. The construction work followed strict rules: a chequerboard street grid, a maximum street width of 22 metres, buildings two storeys high at most. The siting of the school, church and pubs – the last-named always at street corners to make entering and leaving easier – was laid down precisely. A look at Křižíkova ulice demonstrates clearly how the architecture changed in the course of the long construction period. Walk along it from the Negrelli Viaduct – one of Europe's longest bridges in its day – to see how the classical-style buildings slowly transform into Art Nouveau, around where you reach Lyčkovo náměstí.

The communist period, when Karlín deteriorated badly, is thus a historical anomaly. In the late 1990s project developers began to reconstruct the old industrial buildings, for instance at Křižíkova 36a. This attracted better-off citizens to Karlín. Paradoxically, the exceptional floods of 2002, which damaged many buildings, accelerated its gentrification: long-standing residents with little money moved out, and a few protected heritage buildings were, shamefully, demolished. Unenlightened urban planners were involved in this – but that's another story.

Address Karlín, 180 00 Prague 8 | Getting there Metro B, C to Florenc, then go along the streets Ke Štvanici and Křižíkova, and under the Negrelli Viaduct | Tip There are many places to eat and drink in Karlín. One of the most original cafés is Divoké matky, ("Wild Mothers"), at Hybešova 2. If the name doesn't tell you what kind of customers are intended, here is the unofficial motto: "Wild mothers – for you and your brats!"

45 _ The Karlov Church

Conspicuous but forgotten

For years now, the marketing business has been trying to divert the gaze of drivers heading for Prague city centre at the end of the gigantic Nusle Bridge towards an enormous advertising display – but in vain. Most drivers look across to the majestic dome of the church at Karlov, rather than reading the flashing advertisements.

However, most citizens of Prague know little or nothing about Karlov's Church of the Ascension of the Virgin and Emperor Charlemagne, architecturally one of the most remarkable places of worship in Prague. Charles IV ordered its construction, taking as a model the palace chapel of Charlemagne in Aachen, which explains the octagonal ground plan, an unusual feature in a Gothic building. The original vaulting has not survived, but the more recent star-shaped rib vaulting dating from 1575, which according to legend was constructed with assistance from the devil, is guaranteed to take your breath away. The church became famous for its image of the pregnant Virgin Mary. In the 18th century this painting was a destination for, above all, female pilgrims; Empress Maria Theresa had a copy of it hung in her bedroom. This proved effective: she gave birth to 16 children.

Perhaps the church is so little known because it's not open to visitors at all times. It has no permanent parish office and is looked after by a deacon, Jiří Ignác Laňka, who is also the chief trainer of the anti-terrorist unit of the Czech police. It's only open for church services or cultural events, and for guided tours about three times a month. Don't miss this two-hour tour. Michal Soukup, a fervent admirer of this church, will tell you the legend of the builder while spicing up his commentary with sighs about "this absolutely hideous postmodern world" – in English, if requested. After all, an extraordinary church deserves a highly unusual church guide.

Address Ke Karlovu 453/1, 120 00 Prague 2, www.kostelnakarlove.com | **Getting there** Metro C to I. P. Pavlova, then bus 148 to Dětská nemocnice Karlov and left into Ke Karlovu | **Hours** Irregular – see website | **Tip** The original painting of the pregnant Virgin Mary is not far away in the Church of St Apollinaris, which is open for Mass (Mon, Wed, Fri 7.45am, Thu 6.30pm, Sun 11.15am). It was taken there during the Josephine reforms, and the parish is unwilling to return it.

46 The Kiosk

Prague's gingerbread house

Grabbing a newspaper on the way to work – for many people this is part of the daily routine. If you do this at the tram stop at the central station, you can get your newspaper in a genuinely unique place. Since the 1920s this has been the site of what is probably the sole surviving newspaper kiosk in the Rondo-Cubist style, a variety of Cubism that enlivens the austere Cubist geometry by means of decorative arches.

The red and white wooden kiosk looks like many people's idea of a gingerbread house. It could take its place in a fairy tale by virtue of its size, too, as only two or three customers can squeeze inside it at one time.

The identity of the architect of this charming newsstand is unknown. Some say it's the work of Pavel Janák, a theorist of Cubism who also designed the Rondo-Cubist Adria Palace, as the kiosk resembles some of his sketches. Others draw attention to its similarity to the small buildings that Josef Gočár designed for Praha-Kbely Airport. Yet others point out that the Prague municipal government always employed its own architects for small utilitarian structures, and in fact the names of Gočár and Janák were first mentioned in connection with the kiosk only in 1980, when it was scheduled for demolition, and Prague's conservationists began a campaign to save it. A year later it was listed as protected heritage, and restored.

In 2008 the kiosk was repainted in its original colours. But it didn't remain free of graffiti for long, which rather spoils the fairy-tale impression. Too bad: after all, this gingerbread house doesn't stand in the middle of a dark forest, but at the edge of a notorious park, Vrchlické sady. In the 1990s this was given the nickname "Sherwood" by the people of Prague, due to frequent robberies and a generally bad reputation. But that's a different tale. And the kiosk, at least, lived happily ever after.

Address Corner of Bolzanova and Opletalova, 110 00 Prague 1 | Getting there Tram 5, 9, 15, 26 to Hlavní nádraží | Hours Mon–Fri 10am–10pm, Sat & Sun 2–10pm | Tip Close to the kiosk stands the statue *Sbratření*, meaning "fraternisation," on which a partisan and a Red Army soldier are shown in an embrace that's almost passionate. This is a copy of a sculpture by Karel Pokorný dating from the 1950s; the original is in Česká Třebová.

tabák
A
MINISTERSTVO ZDRAVOTNICTVÍ VARUJE:
KOUŘENÍ ZPŮSOBUJE RAKOVINU.
KUPÓNY MHD
YELAS
ILL

47 _ Klamovka

A hidden-away pub

The writer Angelo Maria Ripellino describes the city of Prague as "magical" – and when the balmy air beneath the chestnut trees attracts you into the Klamovka garden restaurant, you have to agree with him. Yet this enchanted spot also labours under a historic curse.

The park and the original Baroque manor house were built in the 18th century by the noble Clam-Gallas family, which is the reason for the name "Klamovka." About 100 years later the mayor of Košíře bought the mansion, and paid for the construction of an electric tramway from Anděl, with the intention of tempting as many diners as possible to his new garden restaurant. The project ended in financial disaster, and the mayor killed himself. When his son took over the business, things continued to go awry: at the opening of the park's zoo, a bear broke free from its chains and tore a small child limb from limb.

Today Klamovka is known above all as the unofficial centre of the Prague dissidents of the 1980s. Above the bar counter, a photograph of the Madonna of Košíře watches over proceedings. This portrait of a mysterious lady, discovered by the legendary landlord of the pub, became the logo of the illegal journal *Revolver Revue*, which circulated as a samizdat publication. The original portrait was stolen in 1995, and the high rent then forced the landlord to give up the business.

Today Klamovka has been renovated and is a typical Czech pub. Sometimes the new owner puts on concerts by unknown bands, or holds events such as hog roasts or kick boarding for children. The characteristic charm of the pub has something to do with the service, which can be slow and truculent – as if the curse still lay upon Klamovka. But that's no reason not to go there: the pub may be hidden away, but a drink in the beer garden in summer has a lot to recommend it. You could say there's a certain magic in the air.

Address Klamovka 2051, 150 00 Prague 5, www.zahradnirestaurace.cz | **Getting there** Tram 9, 10, 15, 16, 21 or Bus 123, 143, 167, 191 to Klamovka. The entrance to the park is opposite the bus stop, the pub another 100 metres further up | **Hours** Daily 11am–midnight | **Tip** There are several equestrian monuments in Prague. The one in Klamovka is well worth seeing, as it is dedicated solely to a horse, the favourite mount of a member of the Clam-Gallas family. The column with the horse's head is on the left, a few steps from the park entrance.

48 Langhans House
From negatives to positives

Normally a negative is the source of a positive. Here, by contrast, what happened in the 20th century went from the positive to the negative. How could that happen?

In 1880, Jan Langhans opened a portrait studio that grew into the biggest photography company in Bohemia. What distinguished it from the others was that Langhans not only took photographs, but also carefully archived all of his negatives. Thanks to this, his customers could see how they themselves had once looked, and also behold their revered ancestors. For portraits of well-known subjects, such as the king of England or the shah of Persia, Langhans kept a special register, the "gallery of famous people." In 1948 the studio was nationalised, and the archive of glass negatives was thrown on to a rubbish dump near Prague. This was the beginning of the negative times.

Everything turned positive again after 1989, when the building was returned to Langhans' heirs. They restored it, retaining its architectural features and adding something else: an apartment with large areas of glass and striking copper shutters. The depth of the house is surprising: a long corridor next to Foto Škoda, a shop that's a Mecca for Prague's photographers, leads to a quiet courtyard. Here you'll find a gallery and a café, whose existence is quite unsuspected by most passers-by. Both are run by an NGO called People In Need.

In this corridor is a photo of an old cupboard that stood neglected for decades next to the boiler room. When the building workers opened it, they revealed the greatest sensation of modern Czech photography. It contained part of the "gallery of famous people" – more than 9,000 glass negatives that, by some miracle, had survived the orgy of destruction carried out in the 1950s. At present they are undergoing restoration, with the purpose of making them available for public viewing.

LANGHANS

Address Vodičkova 37, 110 00 Prague 1, www.langhans.cz | **Getting there** Metro A, B to Můstek, exit to Václavské náměstí; tram 3, 5, 6, 9, 14, 24 to Václavské náměstí | **Hours** Mon–Sat 10am–8pm | **Tip** The Styl & Interier café next door is delightful.

49 Letná

Bohemian life in Prague's Montmartre

When the Academy of Art moved into its new building in the Letná district in the early 20th century, painters and sculptors soon followed. Studios appeared in attics and back yards, cafés and pubs, on the ground floors of houses. This Bohemian quarter between two parks was given the nickname "Prague's Montmartre."

Though you'll no longer find artists' studios here today, the Bohemian atmosphere remains: Letná is turning into a trendy hipster quarter. The residents of the houses built in Art Nouveau, Neo-Renaissance and Functionalist styles love their neighbourhood, and meet in pubs and cafés that have lots of character. Inside, discussions, seminars and exhibitions take place; outside, people drink in backyard beer gardens. It's the perfect recommendation for a relaxed afternoon.

Start off with a cup of coffee at Nacafe, which is really cosy, with lots of books and magazines. At Alchymista, with its 1920s retro-style, they serve a famous cake named after the café, and have one of Prague's most romantic beer gardens. You can eat well at the art academy's Klub AVU, which is not restricted to students. Signs with the laconic lettering *Klub* direct you to a plain room in the basement. The chef here used to work in the Michelin-starred restaurant Alcron, and the food is outstanding.

To round things off, the best option is to drink beer at the intimate Café Lajka. In summer the big windows are thrown wide open and the customers sitting at the bar (which was cobbled together from grandma's sideboard) include not only students from the academy opposite, but also employees of anti-corruption organisations in which two of the café owners work. If you haven't yet breathed enough creative air, the Fraktal a Vegtral restaurant, Těsně vedle Burundi pub and Záletná sova bar await your visit. We confidently predict that one afternoon will not be enough.

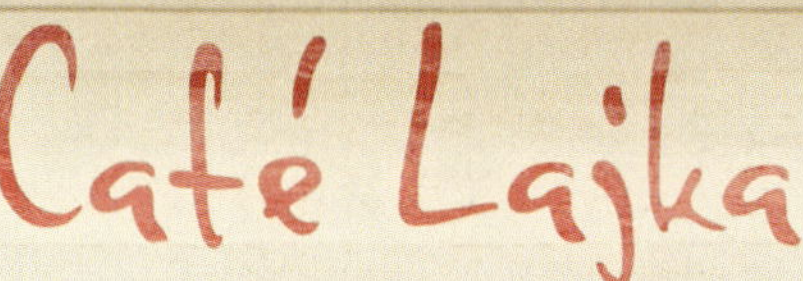

Address Nacafe: Šmeralova 15, www.nacafe.cz; Alchymista: Jana Zajíce 7, www.alchymista.cz; Klub AVU, U Akademie 4, www.facebook.com/KlubAVU; Café Lajka: U Akademie11, www.cafelajka.cz, 170 00 Prague 7 | **Getting there** Tram 1, 8, 12, 25, 26 to Letenské náměstí | **Hours** Nacafe: Mon–Sun noon–10pm; Alchymista: Mon–Fri 7.30am–9.30pm, Sat & Sun 10am–9.30pm; Klub AVU: Mon–Fri 9am–10.30pm; Café Lajka: Mon–Fri 10am–10pm, Sat & Sun noon–10pm | **Tip** If you like cake and enjoy good, healthy eating and drinking in green surroundings, go to the Vozovna Stromovka restaurant. It's situated in a former tram depot and has a children's playground.

50 Libri Prohibiti

The house of forbidden books

At the entrance you take off your coat and sign the register, then all you have to do is ask a member of the staff to fetch the work that interests you from the book stacks. A typical academic library.

Only at a second glance does it become clear how remarkable this institution is. It is the only entirely private library in the Czech Republic that's open to everyone. You will look in vain for a sign on the house to tell you that the third floor is a place of resort for bibliophiles. But this in no way diminishes the importance of the holdings: Libri Prohibiti has tens of thousands of books, magazines and audio or video recordings that could be subsumed under the somewhat vague term "samizdat." It wasn't by any means solely anti-communist publications that were unwelcome to the regime – even *Lord of the Rings* was privately printed, perhaps because the censors objected to the locating of Mordor in the east.

The origins of the library are also interesting. One of the people who used to place layers of paper interspersed with carbon paper in his typewriter was its later founder, Jiří Gruntorád. Before the fall of communism, he produced a samizdat publication that had the witty name *Popelnice* – meaning "rubbish bin." Immediately after the revolution he considered what he should do with its archive and his own collection of prohibited writings. First he offered it all to established institutions, but in vain. This would probably have led to the collection being placed in holdings that were not accessible: what the communists tried unsuccessfully to achieve would then, paradoxically, have happened in the era of freedom. Then, thanks to the support of many people, including Václav Havel, he founded a library that is open to all. Unless you're there for an exhibition opening or a concert, please obey the library rules. Restrictions still apply.

Address Senovážné náměstí 2, 110 00 Prague 1, www.libpro.cz | **Getting there** Metro A, B to Můstek (get out at Václavské náměstí), then any tram to Jindřišská | **Hours** Mon–Thu 1–5pm | **Tip** At Jindřišská 14 there's another place closely linked to the written word. In this post office you can post your letters 22 hours a day, from 2am until midnight, in the beautiful Neo-Renaissance style covered hall. Historic P.O. boxes can be seen in the first-floor passage around the hall.

51 The Lime Kilns

A stone giant on the edge of the city

Here you don't feel you're merely on the edge of the city – but at the end of the world. The lime kilns stand next to a decaying guesthouse on a deserted road between two outlying districts of Prague, Velká Chuchle and Slivenec. The distance from the nearest bus stop may be only one kilometre, but few tourists find their way here. However, if you're keen on "technological sightseeing" or the beauty of 19th century industrial buildings, do not fail to visit the kilns.

The site has been described as an industrial sculpture, and with good reason. With its four towers it's reminiscent of a bizarre steamship that's landed here from Karel Zeman's fantastical world of film. Some people are reminded of bottles of champagne in wine coolers.

The lime kilns have a special significance in the history of technology: they were built in the second half of the 19th century according to a revolutionary process patented by Professor Jiří Pacold that made it possible to use all types of limestone, without sorting, before it was burned in the kiln.

Stone from the nearby quarry was burned here until 1938, but then the buildings became dilapidated. Although the site was declared to be a "technical heritage" even before the fall of the communist regime, it was touch and go whether it would fall into ruin. The process of decay was assisted by the local population, who busily exploited the kilns as a source of bricks.

However, there were also enthusiasts who sacrificed their leisure time to rescue this industrial curiosity. This delighted one of the descendants of the original owners, who decided to restore the lime kilns with aid from the city government, following restitution. At present he's less pleased about the presence of geocachers and the operators of drones, whose toys have to be extracted from the towers from time to time by means of a crane.

Address Pacoldova vápenka, V dolích 205, 159 00 Prague 5 | **Getting there** Metro B to Smíchovské nádraží, then bus 244 to Závodiště Chuchle and bus 172 to Velká Chuchle; from there go up the main road | **Hours** Always open, but a fence blocks direct access to the kilns | **Tip** About 250 metres below the kilns, at a sign marked *Přírodní památka*, a narrow path goes uphill on the left. After a steep ascent (keep left where the path forks) you'll get a remarkable view of the kilns and a panorama across the countryside.

52 The Log Cabin
A mountain idyll in the heart of the city

In the Alps or the Dolomites no one would be surprised. But it's remarkable to find a log cabin, of all things, in the lower part of Vinohrady, practically in the city centre. Alpine charm in the midst of tenements and modern buildings – how did that happen?

Even back in 1921–22, when Josef Janeček, the director of the mine in Kladno, built this house, the Alpine style was thought strange. At that time Královské Vinohrady, the fourth largest city in Bohemia, was in the process of merging with Prague. It's no longer known what inspired Janeček to construct the cabin, but immediately after its completion he sold it to the industrialist Richard Dubský, the great uncle of the present owner.

Of course it's not a modest little hut, but a three-storey wooden house with red window frames, about 20 rooms and a basement. In World War II it served as accommodation for the Hitler Youth, and afterwards it was a residence of Charles University, for prominent students from Saudi Arabia and Africa. Later it was occupied by the offices of the Prognostics Institute of the Academy of Sciences, and the Economics University. Today the house is privately owned again, so unfortunately the public can see neither the carved hearts that adorn the balustrade nor the wooden radiator covers.

It's also doubtful whether it will be possible in the future to see the villa from the street. Today it helps to create the romantic atmosphere of the Nusle Steps, which are framed by a green balustrade, trees and a small square from which trainspotters can observe the engines passing through the Vinohrad tunnels. The owner would like to use the wild part of the garden above the villa to build a large house. This would, admittedly, bring in money for essential renovation work on the decaying structure. But then the spirit of the place would be lost forever.

Address Pod Zvonařkou 1746/7 or Pod Nuselskými schody 1746/7, 120 00 Prague 2 | **Getting there** Tram 6, 11, 13 to Nuselské schody | **Tip** On the other side of the Nusle Steps stands a tiny Baroque chapel dedicated to the Holy Family, dating from 1755. In the 20th century it was so dilapidated that it was scheduled for demolition. It was saved with the help of volunteers, and restored by the Old Catholic Church. Mass is celebrated each Thursday at 6pm.

53 — The Luxury Villas
From mud to luxury

When Karel Čapek moved to Vinohrady in 1924, he described the district as a "muddy suburb." People would laugh at this today – it's now one of the most prestigious places in Prague. The high-class residential quarter between Vinohrady and Vršovice is also a sight for sore eyes for all lovers of architecture. Many artists of the first half of the 20th century lived here in fine style.

Start your walk in the street called Bratří Čapků at numbers 28 and 30, where the architect Ladislav Machoň built a house in two halves, for the writer Karel Čapek and his equally well-known brother Josef. You can identify the plain, ivy-covered building by its memorial plaque, which bears portraits of the two brothers.

Josef lived on the left, and the sign *Dr. Karel Čapek* still hangs by the bell at the right-hand entrance.

Walk along Vlašimská and Benešovská to quiet Hradešínská, where you'll get an unusual view of the city. Pause for a moment in front of house number 32, where the architect František Albert Libra lived. Between 1921 and 1924 he designed a complex of 16 detached and 17 semi-detached houses, named Svoboda Colony, in Hradešínská and Na Šafránce. You can recognise Libra's houses by their triangular gables, striking window frames and colour – yellow or ochre.

The villa of the architect Jan Kotěra at Hradešínská 6 makes a completely different impression: this building, with its unwelcoming geometric appearance, has an eye-catching tower with staircase. The arch above the entrance only adds to its appeal.

At Slovenská 4 you can admire the Art Nouveau villa and studio of the sculptor Ladislav Šaloun, the creator of the Jan Hus Monument on Old Town Square. Šaloun is said to have held occult séances in the basement. Today this house, which dates from 1912, is used by the Academy of Art; it is accessible to the public once a year on European Heritage Day.

Address Start at Ulice Bratří Čapků 28 & 30, 100 00 Prague 10, then see description | **Getting there** Tram 10, 16 to Orionka, then walk along Korunní, Šrobárova and Vlašimská to Ulice Bratří Čapků | **Tip** The city government has bought the right-hand half of the semi-detached house at Bratří Čapků 28, once the home of Karel Čapek, and is preparing to open it to the public. Until it does, www.praha10.cz/capek has a virtual tour of Čapek's study, and the room in which the famous Friday group met for their intellectual discussions.

54 Malá Strana Cemetery

Resurrected

Plzeňská is Prague's longest street, and it has the highest concentration of exhaust fumes. On either side of the tramlines, two lanes of traffic roar along – and in the middle of all this is the cemetery of Mala Straná.

Surprising as it may seem, this place of burial is a green oasis where indefatigable ivy clings to the gravestones of famous and long-forgotten citizens of Prague. In the stress of daily life, few people find their way here, and many do not know the cemetery at all. Although it's situated in the Smíchov quarter, it's called the Malá Strana cemetery, because from 1786 to 1884 it was the official burial place for that district and for the Hradčany. Since then sections of it have been sacrificed several times to construct neighbouring buildings, and even in its smaller form it only survived because in 1910 the writer Jakub Arbes campaigned to save it. But things still weren't good, as the city authorities failed to look after it, and the cemetery suffered from vandalism. Restoration of graves dating from the 19th century – most of them signed – did not begin until after 1989, and today the Association for the Preservation of Malá Strana Cemetery is working to renovate it and make the people of Prague appreciate it again.

The cemetery is dominated by a monumental statue of the kneeling Count Thun-Hohenstein. Other famous citizens of Prague were laid to rest here, for example the Dušeks, friends of Mozart from nearby Bertramka. In one of the tombs lies a Prague legend: three-year-old Anna Degenová, said to be a saint who was mistakenly given the soul of an angel before her birth. On earth she helped everyone, even if they abused her kindness. Finally God acknowledged that to live with an angel's heart was too great a burden, and called little Anna back to his side. Unlike the cemetery, she will not be brought back to life.

Address lzeňská, 150 00 Prague 5, www.malostranskyhrbitov.cz | **Getting there** Metro B to Anděl, then tram 9, 10, 15, 16, 21 to Bertramka; the entrance is directly below | **Hours** Nov–Feb 9am–5pm; Mar, Apr, Oct 9am–6pm; May–Sept 9am–7pm | **Tip** In an inconspicuous house at Holečkova 49, 250 metres from the cemetery, the private gallery Futura opens from Wed to Sun. Here you can see exhibitions by contemporary Czech and international artists, as well as a provocative installation by David Černý in the garden.

55 Malvazinky

Honey, I shrunk the houses!

If you've taken a fancy to the colourful little houses in the Golden Lane in the castle grounds, we've got a tip for you. There's an area of communal housing off the beaten tourist track that's every bit as small and picturesque, where tranquillity and cosiness reign. Welcome to Malvazinky.

In contrast to the world-famous tourist attraction at the Hradčany, the houses here do not cling to the wall, but have tiny front and back gardens. Moreover, they cover a larger area, a total of five streets, which are connected in a few places by alleys. The estate consists of two parts. One is bounded by the streets Přímá, Konečná, Xaveriova and U Smíchovského hřbitova, while the second is just a few steps away in Malá Xaveriova, Xaveriova and Pravoúhlá.

Each house occupies a plot measuring 3.5 by 7 metres; a living room on the ground floor, two tiny bedrooms on the first floor – and that has to suffice. Many of them have a cellar. The estate is very well conserved, which is a unique feature. Even though you'll notice a few plastic windows here and there, most of the houses have been restored with great sensitivity, and the new rendering, painted in delicate pastel tones, suits them extremely well. Here and there behind the diminutive windows you'll see a cup or, a vase of flowers, and wreaths in keeping with the season of the year hang on the doors – it's the epitome of a doll's-house residential quarter.

Very little is known about the origins of this estate – only that the local government built it in the 1920s to accommodate people living on a low income. Today it can no longer be described as a poor district. On the other hand, Malvazinky is far from being a hip or gentrified quarter. In 2015 a house with 75 square metres of living space was sold for a price of approximately 4.5 million Kč – just £140,000. So what are you waiting for?

Address Start: U Smíchovského hřbitova, 150 00 Prague 5, then see description | **Getting there** From the Na Knížecí tram stop on Smíchovské nádraží, take bus 134 to Malvazinky, then continue 200 metres along U Smíchovského hřbitova | **Tip** Exactly halfway between the two parts of the estate, the charming cake shop Snídejte šampaňské serves exactly what its name says —champagne for breakfast – but also delicious cakes and freshly-made filled rolls.

56_ The MeetFactory
Culture made flesh

The influence that the artist David Černý has had on the appearance of Prague during the past 25 years is truly unbelievable: the horse that hangs upside down in the Lucerna Arcade and the sculpture of Franz Kafka near Národní třída are just two examples of his work. But David Černý has made many more installations for other public spaces in the city, and some tour companies even offer special guided tours of Černý's works.

These excursions often conclude at the MeetFactory, where some visitors apparently expect to find a museum of the artist's work. Their disappointment doesn't last long, however. Some years ago, David Černý established a multifunctional space in this industrial building wedged between an urban highway and a railway line. It includes three galleries, an open-air exhibition space on one of the façades, a theatre and a large multi-purpose room, normally used for concerts. On the ceiling is highly original soundproofing in the form of upturned seats that were formerly in the Lucerna cinema. It's also worth taking a look at the bar, made from reinforced concrete supports left over after the construction of the Mrázovka Tunnel.

The other floors, where glass and diesel engines were once made, are devoted to a generous programme for artists-in-residence, which more than 30 foreign artists take part in each year. Their work can be viewed in solo exhibitions or in their studios, which are open to the public several times a year as part of the Open Studios project.

If you would like to see some of David Černý's work, take a look at the cars above the entrance, which are reminiscent of meat hanging in an abattoir. As with the name of the whole institution, this is a creative reference to the location that was originally intended for it, the former meat collective in Holešovice, a plan that collapsed after the great floods of 2002.

Address Ke Sklárně 3213/15, 150 00 Prague 5, www.meetfactory.cz | **Getting there** Metro B to Smíchovské nádraží, then tram 4, 5, 12, 20 to Lihovar, then walk out of the city along the tracks, across the bridge and turn right into Ke Sklárně | **Hours** Daily 1–8pm, depending on the evening programme | **Tip** If you haven't had enough of meat, go to the Serbian restaurant Jelica (Na Zlíchově 35). Even vegetarians leave satisfied, as in addition to excellent *pljeskavica*, *ražnjići* and *cevapčići* they have a wide range of raw food. The low-priced midday menu is served until 4pm on weekdays.

57 __ The Memorial of Silence
The platform with destination death

The station in Bubny is a small one, as if from days gone by. Because of the extension of the metro and the roads, it's gradually losing its purpose. However, its tragic history might prevent its demolition: between 1941 and 1945, deportation trains left from here for the ghetto of Theresienstadt and the concentration camps. Of the 50,000 Jews who waited on the platform with their baggage, 90 per cent never returned.

For a long time only historians and descendants of the deported knew that in this building, which survives in its original condition, the Jews of Prague said their last farewells. There wasn't even a memorial plaque. It was not until the 1980s that the Memorial of Silence, an exhibition and education centre about the Holocaust, was established. It serves as a memorial to the silent city through which trainloads of people passed in broad daylight, accompanied only by the gendarmerie.

Aleš Veselý was transported along with his father and sister. His monumental sculpture was the first part of the monument. In 2015 he unveiled a 20-metre-long piece of track in front of the station building. It rises to heaven like Jacob's Ladder. This sculpture, entitled *Gate of No Return*, stands directly on the path that the Jews took to enter the cattle trucks. In changing exhibitions, photos are projected on to the wall in the darkened station hall showing the deportees, whose life stories will eventually be illustrated in a permanent exhibition.

The land around the station is unused, which contributes to the icy atmosphere of the place. One day, however, the monument will be surrounded by a new office and residential quarter. This may be the reason why it won't be just a reminder of the crimes of the Holocaust, but also a place for dialogue that breaks the silence. After the war, the station in Bubny was also the scene of the brutal deportation of Germans.

Address Bubenská 1, 170 00 Prague 7, www.bubny.org | **Getting there** Metro C to
Vltavská, then take Bubenská; tram 6, 17 to Veletržní palác, then along Veletržní | **Hours**
The Gate of No Return is accessible at all times, the interior only during events | **Tip** On
the site that is now the Parkhotel, Veletržní 1502/20, there once stood wooden pavilions
selling electrical goods. The Jews spent their last days before deportation here. They endured
a protracted registration and humiliating checks on their property. From here they went to
the station. A memorial plaque is attached to a concrete wall in front of the hotel.

58 _ Memorial to the Horror
The glorious seven of the Heydrichiad

18 June, 1942: it is dark, damp and cold. The time is shortly after four in the morning, and seven men are surrounded by hundreds of Gestapo and SS members. Nevertheless, another eight hours will pass before the Nazis storm the crypt of the Cathedral of St Cyril and St Methodius. For more than 20 days, seven Czech and Slovak paratroopers hid here. They had carried out the attack on "the blond beast," Deputy Reich-Protector Reinhard Heydrich, who died later from his injuries.

Today you enter the crypt through a black steel door, and immediately feel closed in. The cramped space with niches on the walls for tombs is now illuminated by light bulbs, but then the paratroopers could only see a few rays of light entering through a small ventilation opening. Bullet holes can be seen on the outside around the window.

A permanent exhibition gives detailed information about the assassination and displays contemporary photographs. The Nazis used machine guns, grenades and tear gas against the rebels; when all of this was ineffective, they flooded the crypt to force the seven to give up. "We will never surrender! We are Czechs!" was the answer. Jan Kubiš, Adolf Opálka and Josef Bublík finally died in an exchange of gunfire in the church; Josef Gabčík, Josef Valčík, Jaroslav Švarc and Jan Hrubý fled to the crypt and shot themselves with their last bullets.

The Czechs have an ambivalent attitude to these heroics: following the attack, the Munich Agreement signed by Britain and France was revoked, but there followed what Czechs call the *Heydrichiad*: brutal retaliatory measures, including the complete destruction of the villages of Lidice and Ležáky. Visitors to the crypt are probably more often tourists than locals. What they find is a moving memorial to the events of World War II – and to the incredible courage of men who did not fear death. It is a place unique in Prague.

Address National memorial for the victims of the Heydrichiad, Resslova 9a (entrance from Na Zderaze), 120 00 Prague 2, www.pamatnik-heydrichiady.cz | **Getting there** Metro B to Karlovo náměstí | **Hours** Mar–Oct, Tue–Sun 9am–5pm; Nov–Feb, Tue–Sat 9am–5pm | **Tip** The residence at Karlovo náměstí 40–41 looks harmless, but it bears the nickname "Faust House" for a reason: in the 16th century the alchemist Edward Kelley carried out experiments here. According to a legend, here Doctor Faustus promised his soul to the devil, who took it to hell through a hole in the ceiling. When the building was renovated after World War II, the skeletons of seven cats were discovered in the foundations.

59___The Model Mine
An underground walk

There are numerous mining museums in different parts of the world. But in a capital city it's unusual to be able to walk through a complex system of mine tunnels, as you can in the Letná district of Prague.

The National Technical Museum has every reason to be proud of its reconstruction of a mine. Since the Middle Ages, mining has played an important role in the lands of Bohemia. The word "dollar" derives from the German word *Joachimsthaler* (*thaler* for short – in Czech *tolar*), a coin that was struck in Bohemia in the early 16th century.

The mine is on two levels, and was already planned when the museum was built. During the German occupation, construction came to a stop. Then the communists continued the project in the 1950s. Their idolisation of miners, who represented the proletarian ideal in their eyes, is one reason why this mine was constructed. It was also intended to attract prospective miners, which is why modern machines were exhibited. The machinery was supplied from the USA and Great Britain as part of postwar aid, but in practice was never put into operation.

A few years ago the exhibition underwent a thorough overhaul. Since then, visitors have no longer gone down the shaft in a lift cage, and no longer see working machines. All the same, the experience that they have is no less powerful. A realistic impression is created by large-scale video projections and authentic sounds, plus 38 figures of miners who are placed in all parts of the mine. The well-informed guides may not have laboured at a coal face, but they can answer all kinds of questions and accompany visitors on the 400-metre circuit of the iron-ore and coal mine – often taking longer than the official 40 minutes. This is not to say that you will not be eager to see daylight again at the end of the tour. But you certainly won't be bored during the time you spend underground.

Address Národní technické muzeum, Kostelní 42, 170 78 Prague 7, www.ntm.cz | **Getting there** Tram 1, 8, 12, 25, 26 to Letenské náměstí, then along Nad Štolou, Letohradská and Muzejní in the direction of Letenské sady | **Hours** Tue – Fri 9.30am – 5.30pm, Sat, Sun & public holidays 10am – 6pm, guided tours every 30 minutes | **Tip** Opposite the museum in the Letenské sady park is a small round building containing the oldest surviving carousel in Europe. A public collection was organised to save and restore it. If we're lucky, this unique and romantic item of technology will soon be open to the public again.

60 The Mushroom Box

An ode to the Czech equivalent of golf

The Czechs are one of the least religious peoples on the planet. Nevertheless, Prague possesses a small statue that is revered by Catholics all over the world – the Infant Jesus of Prague. But opposite the Church of Our Lady Victorious with its famous statue there is another place, not at all conspicuous and quite profane, that characterises the Czechs much better than religious symbols.

Hidden in a passageway through a house, there is something on the wall on the right that you will see nowhere else: a mushroom box. If you're wondering what it's for, then you're probably not a local, and so are unaware that the Czechs are extremely passionate gatherers of mushrooms. Many of them pursue this pastime at least once a year. Even people with no culinary interest go hunting for mushrooms, in the way that other people play golf – because it's a good reason for taking exercise in fresh air.

If you want to know more about what you've gathered, simply put the fungus in the box behind the wooden door and fill in some basic information on a form. After that you can look forward to receiving an email from the Czech Society for Mycology telling you what kind of mushroom it is and whether it's edible.

There's also an advice bureau, the first institution of its kind in the world, which can help during opening hours. One of its founders, the legendary mycologist František Smotlacha, has personally tested the edibility of 1,700 kinds of mushroom.

The box was the idea of the son of the house's owner and the granddaughter of Smotlacha, who continues in the family tradition in her role as an expert on fungi that attack wood. The box was not installed at the request of collectors, but because they used to take their mushroom samples to the offices of the Society for Mycology on the first floor; since a burglary in 2006 the door to the stairs has been kept locked.

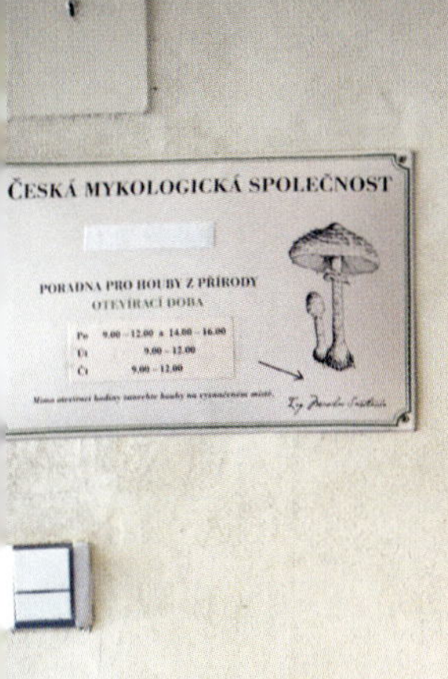

Address Česká mykologická společnost, Karmelitská 14, 118 00 Prague 1, www.myko.cz | **Getting there** Tram 12, 15, 20, 22 to Hellichova | **Hours** Mon – Fri 9am – 6.30pm | **Tip** If you don't feel like eating mushrooms, try the Café de Paris brasserie at Maltézské náměstí 4 and order the house entrecote from the regular menu – you won't regret it.

61 __ Na kopci

Chef, waiter, Michelin

Enthusiasm, hard work, and above all courage: you need all of these things if you want to open a top-class restaurant outside the city centre, serviced by a single bus route.

That's how far off the beaten track Na kopci is. The restaurant was founded in 2006 by the chef Titus Eliáš and waiter Jan Turek. Both of them had gained experience in the kitchen of the famous TV chef Zdeněk Pohlreich. The result is an outstanding combination of high-quality food and drink, pleasant service and an interior that makes you forget straight away the ugliness of the building in which you're sitting.

You dine on the ground floor of one of those prefabricated blocks that socialist urban planners dropped like rectangular concrete excrement into the housing estates. They were supposed to serve as "communal infrastructure," which could mean anything at all. This one was occupied by a butcher's shop and a small grocery. As the building was constructed like a concrete bunker, no major alterations were possible, but Eliáš and Turek exerted themselves all the more to give the restaurant an inviting appearance by other means. They papered the walls with their own homemade wall coverings – photo collages from family albums – which create an intimate atmosphere.

You won't pay any more attention to the decoration as soon as the first course reaches the table. We highly recommend beginning the meal with the "chef starter selection," and are happy to leave the rest to you. The menu changes three or four times a year, but a permanent fixture is the famous steak tartare. Even if prices have risen since the opening, Na kopci provides excellent value for money by Prague's standards. It's not only local gourmets who've made their way up the hill: Michelin inspectors also came and awarded the restaurant a Bib Gourmand in 2015. Who says it doesn't pay to be courageous?

Address K Závěrce 2774/20, 150 00 Prague 5, www.nakopci.com | **Getting there** Metro B to Anděl, from there to Na Knížecí, then bus 231 to Kesnerka | **Hours** Mon–Fri 11.30am–2.30pm and 5.30–11pm, Sat & Sun 11.30am–11pm | **Tip** We recommend two walks to digest your meal: close to the restaurant in U Starého židovského hřbitova you can look over the wall of the Old Jewish Cemetery, founded in 1788. A longer walk goes in the opposite direction: along U Dívčích hradů and then on a path leading to the Ctirad nature monument, from where you'll have an interesting view of Prague.

62 __ Náplavka

A trendy scene by the Vltava

On a hot summer evening, what more could you want than to chill out on the waterside with a glass of beer? For a long time this was hardly possible in the centre of Prague. While people in other cities played, partied and relaxed on the river bank, the Vltava waterfront in the centre of Prague was built up and a little down-at-heel. But that has changed.

On Náplavka, the paved riverbank directly below the Rašín quay, ships once moored, and raftsmen and sand merchants unloaded their wares. After these trades ceased to exist, the area was empty, a place for parked cars and people walking their dogs. In 2007 a citizens' initiative organised an exhibition – and in this way sparked off a transformation. A year later the first concerts were held; a season after that, the first beer garden opened up. Today, on balmy summer evenings, anything is possible here – except sleepy tranquillity. Hundreds of people stroll along the Vltava, go to exhibitions, listen to bands or dance in front of a DJ's stand.

The paved waterfront is part of the river embankment and stands under water when the Vltava floods. For this reason no permanent restaurants have been set up here. The stalls and bars occupy former storage spaces in the embankment wall. One well-known place is Bajkazyl, a repair shop and hire station for bicycles plus a bar, all in one. You can also enjoy yourself down on the water, for example with an evening meal on board the ship *Kristian Marco*, theatre on *Tajemství bratří Formanů*, or an exhibition, concert or reading on the *(A)void* Floating Gallery.

You're not a party person? You'll like Náplavka all the same: since 2010 a farmers' market has taken place here every Saturday morning, when there's a bustle around the fruit, vegetable and meat stalls. If you're looking for a place that the people of Prague have made their own, you've found it here.

Address Rašínovo nábřeží, 120 00 Prague 2, www.farmarsketrziste.cz/naplavka, www.prazskenaplavky.cz/naplavky/rasinovonabrezi | **Getting there** Metro B to Karlovo náměstí, take the exit towards Palackého náměstí and go down the steps at the Palacý Bridge | **Hours** Most bars open daily Apr–Oct, some ships all year round; farmers' market Sat 8am–2pm | **Tip** More steps go down to Náplavka from Na Výtoni. Note an unusual square structure here with a clock face and a windsock. It measures the water level of the Vltava.

63_ The One-Room Hotel

A luxurious tube in the clouds

If you would like to spend the night in an extraordinary room, there's no better place in Prague than the city's smallest hotel: the One-Room Hotel in the Žižkov TV tower – with a height of 70 metres, the tallest in Prague. The tower has also found its way on to a list of the world's ugliest buildings, in spite of the outsize babies by David Černý that "adorn" it.

Although it's advertised as an apartment, the luxury hotel is in fact more like a so-called junior suite. It actually consists of three rooms, but two of them have no source of natural illumination except for a small skylight. For this reason one of them is a huge dressing room, while the other is said to be a conference room, though it's seldom used for this purpose and is currently a massage room. The space that is the living room and bedroom, as well as the bathroom, is divided from the rest by a glass wall that can be covered, and forms a large, elongated, tube-shaped space with an exclusive character – not only because of its luxurious fittings, but above all on account of the view. Almost the whole outer wall is a single window, from which you have a breathtaking view over the roofs of Žižkov. American guests are said to be disappointed when they learn that the extensive green space on the right is not Prague's Central Park but the city's biggest cemetery, in Olšany. If you want to look out on the historic city centre from this height, all you have to do is descend a few steps to Restaurant Oblaca, where a 360-degree panorama awaits you.

If you opt for an all-inclusive reservation, you can surprise your other half during dinner with a banner unfurled outside the window by a hired climber. Standard messages such as "I love you" are included in the price. But if you would like the banner to read "Sorry, I had no idea that you suffered from vertigo," you'll have to pay extra.

Address Mahlerovy sady 1, 130 00 Prague 3, www.towerpark.cz/hotel+4 | **Getting there** Metro A to Jiřího z Poděbrad, from its north end go along Milešovská straight to the tower | **Hours** Hotel reception open 8am–1am | **Tip** The site that is now a park, Mahlerovy sady, was a Jewish cemetery from 1680. Around 1960 most of it was turned into a park, but the oldest part of the cemetery, near Fibichova, was preserved. You get an unusual view of the TV tower from here.

64 The Orthodox Church

Exotic architecture from Carpathian Ukraine

Can you imagine dismantling a church into its individual parts, taking them hundreds of kilometres and putting them back together again in a different place? And doing that twice? If you can't, take a walk to the Orthodox church that stands, partly concealed by trees, in the Kinský Garden.

Next to this wooden structure with its three towers and a shingle roof, you'll feel as if you were in the Ukrainian countryside. It was there, in the village of Velyki Lučky near Mukatsheve, that the little church was built in the second half of the 17th century. In 1793, due to lack of money, the church was sold and taken to a richer place, Medveďov. From there it made a second journey in 1929, this time more than 600 kilometres, when the inhabitants of Carpathian Ukraine, then part of Czechoslovakia, wanted to donate an example of their folk architecture to Prague. Supervised by a priest, they took the building to pieces, numbered all the parts and transported them to Prague in four special rail trucks.

The church is part of the ethnological collection of the National Museum, but since 2008 it has been run by the Orthodox Church. Mass lasts for two hours, but visitors are allowed briefer visits. The heavy wooden door, where a thick curtain hangs in winter to keep out the cold, leads to a narrow space, part of which used to be reserved for women. Candles burn in the gloom, icons hang from beams, and the smell of a wood-burning stove fills the air. The Romanian hymns and prayers, chanted and spoken by a congregation sometimes of ten, sometimes of fifty, have an almost exotic sound.

The Church of the Holy Archangel Michael remains in its original condition. So far only the roof has been renovated. You might also encounter the two cats which are fed by the priest and by the children who come here. They help to complete the scene of rural Ukraine in the middle of Prague.

Address Chrám sv. archanděla Michaela, Petřínské sady 99, 150 00 Prague 5 | **Getting there** Tram 6, 9,12, 20 to Švandovo divadlo, then go up the hill through the Kinský Garden, or bus 143, 149 to Koleje Strahov, then walk past the hall of residence and downhill through the Kinský Garden | **Hours** Mass: Sun 10am & Mon 8am, otherwise open by arrangement with the priest Andrei Ioan Danciu, Tel. +420/777329275 | **Tip** A walk near the church takes you to a water system on a steep slope, fed through an underground tunnel, with two lakes, a waterfall and a cascade.

65   Our Lady of Exile

Heavenly peace, a heavenly view

The path over the Petřín hill, named after Raoul Wallenberg, the Swedish diplomat who saved thousands of Jews in World War II, seems to follow a contour. If you approach it from the Úvoz road, you have a lovely view of the city. It's even better if you take the inconspicuous, sometimes muddy path up to the walls of the Strahov Monastery. Follow the arrows to the statue of the Virgin Mary of Exile, from where there's a wonderful prospect of Malá Strana, with the towers of the castle of Prague and St Nicholas' Church.

It doesn't occur to many tourists to climb up to the little paved square where the statue stands, so you'll have the view all to yourself, and you'll enjoy truly divine peace if you take a seat on the bench – even though the story of this Virgin Mary was not at all peaceful.

It was inspired by the statue of the Virgin that Jan Jiří Bendl sculpted in the 17th century to express the gratitude of the people of Prague for their good fortune in the war against Sweden. The statue was placed on a column on Old Town Square, but shortly after Czechoslovakia gained its independence in 1918 it was torn down and destroyed by demonstrators, who regarded it as a symbol of domination by the old Hapsburg rulers. Later, Czech emigrants to the USA decided to commission a free copy of it, and collected money for that purpose. The Rome-based sculptor Alessandro Monteleone then created the statue of Our Lady of Exile, and in 1955 it was taken to the monastery at Lisle, near Chicago. Pilgrimages were made to this place to pray for the fall of communism.

The statue did not come to Prague until the 1990s. With hands folded in prayer, the Virgin looks heavenwards and intercedes for mortal humans – as the inscription on the base asks her to do. Prayers for the fall of communism were finally heard, so she has performed at least one recognised miracle.

Address Strahovské nádvoří, 118 00 Prague 1 | Getting there Tram 22 to Pohořelec, then walk to Úvoz street, go right to the Petřín hill, then see text | Tip If you go back down to Úvoz you will pass narrow steps leading steeply up to Loretánská. Locals call the steps the "rumbling iron" after the sound they make if you climb with a heavy tread, especially on the lower part.

66 Palác Lucerna

Prague's first arcade

Most tourists come here to see David Černý's anti-nationalist parody: a horse hanging upside down with St Wenceslas sitting on its stomach. Although, following repeated attacks by vandals, the artist had to shorten the horse's long tongue, this grimacing equestrian statue still has a powerful effect. But it would be a pity to go there only for that reason.

Palác Lucerna was built between 1907 and 1920 by the businessman Vácslav Havel, grandfather of the later President Václav Havel. The name Lucerna, meaning lantern, is said to have been suggested by his wife, who felt that its Modernist façade on Vodičkova ulice resembled one. In constructing it, Havel created the first arcade in Prague, and also the apartments, offices, shops and restaurants that are part of it. It's worth visiting the Kavárna Lucerna café on the first floor, and the cinema with an interior in the so-called third Rococo style. The popular Rockclub was originally a cabaret where Vlasta Burian and the famous comedy duo Voskovec and Werich performed. But the best known part of the complex is in the basement: the multipurpose Great Hall was the largest in Prague for a long time. It was originally intended to be an ice rink, but this failed to happen for technical and financial reasons. Before World War II important conferences were held here. Artists like Josephine Baker took to the stage, and Prague's school pupils celebrated their leaving balls here.

In 1952 Lucerna was nationalised, and although the regime put on many communist events, the people of Prague prefer to remember the concerts by Louis Armstrong, Ella Fitzgerald and the legendary Hungarian beat band Locomotiv GT. This building has a presiding cultural spirit that even the communists couldn't silence. And so it was no coincidence that this was the venue of a big memorial concert to honour Václav Havel after his death.

Address Vodičkova 36, 110 00 Prague 1, www.lucerna.cz | Getting there Metro A to Můstek, exit towards Václavské náměstí, then to Vodičkova ulice | Tip Václav Havel's arcade inspired a number of other architects. As a result, Wenceslas Square is riddled with arcades such as that of Palác Koruna at the lower end of the square, known for its late Art Nouveau decoration and its imposing glass dome.

67 __ Paralelní polis

Atomic bomb in the news

Imagine this: you walk into a café, and in the middle of it is a bar that looks like an ordinary table. "Will I even get served here?" you might ask yourself, but that's not the only thing that's different in this café. Right by the entrance is a machine that changes Kč into bitcoins – the world's newest currency. In contrast to a dollar, euro or Czech crown it has no physical existence, but is purely virtual; the method of payment is similar to using a credit card. The bitcoin machine is easy to use: after pressing the touchscreen a few times, a virtual purse appears on your mobile phone showing the amount you've chosen. If you don't have a smartphone, you can print out the "purse."

Why go to all this trouble? Because it's worth it. For one thing, you can get one of the best cups of coffee in Prague here. And as the bitcoin is a decentralised currency that belongs to neither a country nor a bank, payment with it is practically anonymous. In the café you can experiment to find out how easy it is to operate without institutional control. This is one of the reasons why Paralelní polis was founded. The house with the grey-black façade is home not only to the café, but also to a workshop with 3-D printers, a lecture room and the so-called Institute for Cryptoanarchy – as the hackers, for whom a coworking space is available, like to describe themselves. Most of the furniture in the café and the other rooms is made from honeycomb paper.

The project originated with a group of artists called Ztohoven, who once succeeded in getting a story about an atomic bomb explosion into a live broadcast on Czech television. The law courts acquitted the group of the charge of disseminating fake news. And at Paralelní polis you will realise that there's no reason to be afraid of these hackers, or of the people who are researching alternative ways for society to function.

Address Dělnická 43, 170 00 Prague 7, www.paralelnipolis.cz | **Getting there** Tram 1, 6, 12, 14, 25 to Dělnická, then a short walk towards the Vltava | **Hours** Mon – Fri 8am – 8pm, Sat & Sun 10am – 8pm | **Tip** If you're interested in seeing what kind of devices the hackers and their parents grew up with, visit the little computer museum at Jatečná ulice 33a. It's part of a huge showroom belonging to the Alza.cz electronics company.

68 The Paternoster

A servant from a bygone age

Few things in life evoke such contrasting emotions as a paternoster. Some are afraid that they won't be able to enter or leave, while others wax nostalgic at the sight of one of these rotating elevators. Thrill-seeking teenagers deliberately fail to get out at the top or bottom but stay inside the cabin to see what happens. The age of the paternoster has sadly passed – so come along for a ride before the very last one has ceased to turn.

A paternoster is a system of cabins suspended on two chains that are in permanent motion, in the way that pious Christians used to slip the beads of a rosary through their fingers – and this is the origin of the name, which means "Our Father." The first lift of this kind, powered by steam, was built in the 1880s in England. In Czechoslovakia, the paternoster had its golden age in the 1920s, when many major institutions were created. For buildings in which many people work the paternoster is ideal, because little time is lost in waiting. However, they were gradually removed, as they don't meet modern safety standards. Nevertheless, there's no reason to be afraid, as the paternoster has a sensor that brings it to a stop if anyone gets stuck between the cabin and the walls.

There are still about 20 paternosters in Prague, but only a few of them are accessible to the public. Three remain in the city centre: in the first staircase of Dům U Nováků, which was modelled on Parisian shopping centres; in the government offices of Prague 1; and finally in the Lucerna Arcade, hidden behind a closed-off glass door opposite the entrance to the Great Hall.

So what happens if you ignore all the warning signs and don't get out as your cabin approaches the top floor? Does it turn by 180 degrees and tip you on your head, or does it simply shift sideways? Try it for yourself. We can reveal that every daring teenager has survived the experience.

Address U Nováků: Vodičkova 30; Prague 1 (Úřad městské části Praha 1): Vodičkova 18; Lucerna: Vodičkova 36, 110 00 Prague 1 | **Getting there** Metro A, B to Můstek (exit to Václavské náměstí) | **Hours** U Nováků: Mon–Fri 6am–6pm; city offices: Mon & Wed 8am–7pm, only during office hours; Lucerna: only when visiting the companies that occupy the building | **Tip** On the first floor of the house at Palackého 7 you can visit the original home of the historian František Palacký and his son-in-law František Ladislav Rieger, major figures in the "national reawakening." See www.nm.cz for information and to book in advance.

69 — Pečkárna

House of horror

More than 70 years ago, the name of this house used to arouse indescribable fear. Palác Pečkárna, built by the banker Julius Petschek, was the Gestapo headquarters in Bohemia, and its base in Prague from 1939 to 1945. Today it is the seat of the Ministry of Industry and Trade, and few people know that the cellars in which prisoners awaited interrogation are a place of memorial.

Sadly, the exhibition is not well balanced. It provides little information about the Gestapo or the resistance. The first room is devoted to the Sudetenland, but it doesn't address the question of postwar expulsions. What makes a visit worthwhile are the rooms themselves. Don't expect a pleasant experience. It's dark here, with few windows. The rooms are soundless, with harsh lighting and stale air. Like prisoners in the war years, visitors first enter a room with wooden benches. Here arrested persons often had to spend the whole day in complete silence, staring at a white wall – which is why this room was called "the cinema." Those who spoke were punished by being deprived of food and made to stand for three days.

Opposite were three tiny cells – converted bank safes – where "special cases" were imprisoned. There was hardly room to stand up, and the wooden bunk and narrow passage were illuminated only by a small window. Next door was the interrogation room, which was once on the first floor. The mere sight of the instruments of torture suffices: the wooden post to which prisoners were bound, and the jackets with steel rods that the Nazis put on their victims. These prevented bruises forming when they were beaten, but caused serious internal injuries.

The stories of the people who were interrogated here can make you feel sick, and this uncomfortable feeling might last for some time after you've left the building. The emotions that Pečkárna once evoked are still disturbing.

Address Politických vězňů 20, 110 00 Prague 1 | **Getting there** Metro A, C to Muzeum, then walk along Washingtonova | **Hours** Tours (in Czech only) for five people or more, on open days or by arrangement; contact csbspraha@volny.cz | **Tip** The nuclear bunker of Hotel Jalta (Václavské náměstí 45) was intended to accommodate the emergency staff of the Warsaw Pact states in case of war. Today a group of volunteers have installed the Museum of the Cold War here. See www.muzeum-studene-valky.cz to book a visit.

70 _ The People's Canteen
Welcome to the 1980s

When hamburger and pizza chains came to the Czech Republic in the 1990s, it was the death knell for traditional snack bars. Unfortunately, in these years the legendary Automat Koruna on Wenceslas Square also closed down. Many Prague people still remember it, not only for its strawberry milk shakes and potato fritters but also for the anecdotes, for example that you only had to turn your head, and hey presto! – the sausage had disappeared from your plate.

It's over. The only reminders of the old days are the snack bars in butcher's shops that you'll find in every district of Prague, where you can stand at Formica-topped tables with bricklayers in their working clothes and enjoy tripe soup, roast loin or minced beef. If you would prefer to soak up a more cultivated yet authentically retro atmosphere, go to the People's Canteen in Těšnov.

Don't let the name deceive you. People queue on the pavement around midday every weekday for the food in this restaurant. The customers are not only workers and pensioners, but also managers and other office employees. For 100 Kč they get a three-course meal of unexpectedly high quality. The dishes range from typically Bohemian, for example goulash with potato fritters, to healthier and more modern offerings such as couscous or salad.

The furnishings, by contrast, are anything but modern. The walls of the modest room are covered with brown tiles and dark wood. Net curtains hang at the windows, and lamps dangle from the ceiling between strange-looking wooden beams. On the chequered tablecloths are salt, pepper and sauce. This picture from the 1980s is completed by knives with black plastic handles, and a glass of orangeade for 4 Kč. All that spoils this trip back to the past are the modern screens displaying the day's menu, and the fact that no one is likely to steal the sausage from your plate.

Address Lidová jídelna Těšnov, Těšnov 5, 110 00 Prague 1 | **Getting there** Metro B, C to Florenc, or tram 3, 8, 14, 24 to Bílá labuť | **Hours** Mon – Fri 10.30am – 2pm | **Tip** It's worth visiting the famous snack bar U Rozvařilů on the fifth floor of the Bílá Labuť department store (Na Poříčí 23). In this enormous, half-empty room you are greeted by wine-red tablecloths, somewhat higher prices and signs asking diners in "working clothes" to sit only in the front part of the restaurant.

71_The Police Museum

Tim Burton's chamber of horrors

Have you always dreamed of being a police detective? Would you like to take fingerprints or find clues at the scene of a crime – in a modern, interactive exhibition? If so, the Police Museum of the Czech Republic is not what you're looking for.

Nevertheless, it's well worth a visit. It even has one interactive feature, the police software for creating identikit pictures of suspects. The collections, which are kept in the cloister of a former Augustinian monastery, have a completely different kind of charm. And if you have no interest in reading the lengthy descriptions on the labels of what seem to be thousands of exhibits, you will be astonished simply by the bizarre nature of this institution. Although the permanent exhibition has been rearranged several times since 1989, it seems impossible to exorcise the ghosts of its communist founders.

Take, for example, the uniform of the special police unit that brutally beat up students on 17 November 1989 – presented here without any form of comment. If you enjoy watching horror films, you will surely take pleasure in the recreations of scenes from criminal history using life-sized waxwork figures, which look so macabre that Tim Burton would be proud of them. There is also a very strange section that seems to be pursuing the aim of steering children away from drugs. When you examine this display, it's difficult to avoid speculating about whether the creators themselves were smoking certain illegal substances when they put it together. To round off the exhibition you are permitted to pass through a cut-off traffic barrier, with appropriate sound effects, to enter the other parts of what was once a Gothic-style building.

It doesn't matter that the museum displays are not labelled in English, and that the ticket desk provides nothing more than a few old leaflets. It's quite enough to come and look.

Address Muzeum policie ČR, Ke Karlovu 1, 120 00 Prague 2, www.muzeumpolicie.cz | **Getting there** Metro C to I. P. Pavlova, then bus 148 to Dětská nemocnice Karlov and turn left into Ke Karlovu | **Hours** Tue – Sun 10am – 5pm | **Tip** In Horská there is a fine reconstruction of the Baroque city walls, from where you'll get a wonderful view of Prague.

72_Požáry

A geological and romantic nature reserve

If the soul of a hobo is slumbering inside you, or you're fascinated by the Wild West, there's no better place in Prague than Požáry ("Fires"), a protected natural reserve.

Geologists will find this remote spot particularly interesting. Požáry, once a limestone quarry, is a globally recognised stratotype, i.e. an ideal example of rock layers from a specific geological era. There are only 77 such stratotypes in the world, and three of them are in the Czech Republic. Fans of the early history of the earth as written in stone will be pleased to hear that the site is important for finds of trilobites and other fossils.

Požáry arouses the yearnings of nature lovers – especially those who like the idea of travelling *500 Miles* on *Country Roads* themselves. The entrance alone seems imposing. A little way off the path, you climb steep iron steps and reach a tunnel several metres long. A one-track railway used to pass through it to transport the stone that had been excavated. The front wall of the tunnel bridges a gap between two rocks, and its entrance is a pseudo-Gothic arch, which gives you the feeling that you're entering a forgotten kingdom of the Middle Ages. On the far side you come to the quarry, and behind that a further tunnel leads to the second part of the quarry. This second section has been roughly hewn from the rock, and the end is partially blocked up, so it's advisable to take a flashlight. However, even without one you can admire the rocks around you, from which limestone was extracted until the beginning of World War II.

If all that this place offers doesn't provide enough of the romance of the Wild West for your taste, we cannot unfortunately recommend using any of the fire hearths that are here, because no one could want this place to live up to its name. Nevertheless, there is of course no objection to your singing *Ring of Fire*.

Address Na Požáru, 155 00 Prague 5 | Getting there Metro A to Nemocnice Motol, then Bus 174 to Řeporyjské náměstí, along Dalejská and under the viaduct; just beyond it, through K Holému vrchu and after 650 metres, leave the path on the right by the iron steps | Tip Pay a visit to Kavárna Na náměstí, at Řeporyjské náměstí. It proves that you can have excellent coffee, tasty snacks and pleasant service even on the fringes of the city.

73 Prague Crossroads
Havel, church and culture

It's a fascinating story: how a dissident became head of state and attracted famous people from around the world to Prague, thanks to his charisma. While he was president, Václav Havel received them in the castle, but also showed them more unusual places, as is shown by photos of Bill Clinton playing the saxophone in the Reduta jazz club. After his presidency, Havel most of all liked taking guests to the arts centre in the deconsecrated St Anne's Church. He was the initiator of Pražská křižovatka (Prague Crossroads), where conferences, concerts, exhibitions and political events are held today.

Although this tall Gothic church is in the city centre, it's easily overlooked, as it stands on the site of the former St Anne's Convent, which is run by the National Theatre today. It was the only church in Prague that the Hussites didn't ruin. Some say that nuns from burnt-out convents were interned here, while others claim that the abbess was the aunt of Jan Žižka. Yet others believe that the Hussites wanted to destroy the church, but failed to find the door as the place was so huge. In the 18th century Joseph II ordered it to be deconsecrated. It was then occupied by a printing works and a paper store.

The years of decay continued until Václav and Dagmar Havel's foundation, Vize 97, stepped in. When you enter the church, its dimensions will take your breath away, and it has retained a spiritual atmosphere to this day. On the walls, fragments of medieval frescoes still shimmer, and the Gothic roof floats above your head. In place of an altar, there is a modern stage at the front of the church. References to the memory of Václav Havel, for example the glass totem that is filled with ribbons from the wreaths on his grave, add to an atmosphere that is laden with meaning. This was the place where the people of Prague queued in 2011 to say their farewells to him.

Address Zlatá (entrance from Liliová), 110 00 Prague 1, www.prazskakrizovatka.cz | Getting there Tram 2, 17, 18 to Karlovy lázně, then along Náprstkova and across Betlémské náměstí to Liliová, where you turn left into the alley called Zlatá after a few metres | Hours Only open for events | Tip Vize 97 has preserved the office in which Havel worked after the end of his term as president in virtual form. You can see its original condition at www.vaclavhavel.com. The event videos are free, but you have to pay to take a virtual tour.

74 Pragulic
The other side of the city

You've never had a city guide like this before. He's called Karim, has black make-up around his eyes and carefully varnished nails. He wears clunky rings and slightly threadbare clothes. He is a little over 40, but missing front teeth and hard facial features make him look older. No wonder: he lived on the streets for more than 20 years, mostly surviving by prostitution; for six years he took methamphetamine. Karim is one of the few who has succeeded in breaking out of this vicious circle. Today he works for Pragulic, a social enterprise that presents Prague through the eyes of the homeless.

Pragulic was founded in 2012 by three students. They wanted to help the homeless and enable people to get to know those whom we usually avoid – and at the same time to establish a reputable enterprise. Today Pragulic gives permanent employment to seven city guides; each of them shows you a side of the city that reflects his or her own life: drugs, alcohol, prostitution, gambling addiction and the longing for freedom taken to extremes.

Karim starts his tour at the central station, where he began selling his body at the age of 16. He divides the city into zones: whereas Wenceslas Square is in the hands of various mafia groups, on the Charles Bridge Czech students and single mothers offer themselves for sex. He tells you in which arcade, which rubbish bin or sewer you can spend the night, how much you can earn per day from begging, and where the most corrupt policemen are on the beat. He takes you to Perlová street, once the centre of prostitution, and to the Louvre coffee house, which used to be home to the notorious disco Riviéra, where one of his customers deliberately infected him with HIV. Paradoxically, this helped him to get out of prostitution.

If you know Prague, you'll know many of these places, yet you will feel that you've never really been there before.

Hours Each guide leads several tours per week, with varying meeting places; reservations: www.pragulic.cz. | **Tip** The sex workers of Perlovka (Perlová street), are commemorated by an inconspicuous plaque on the building at the corner of Uhelný trh. It reads: *To the fallen women. Honour their p…*

75   Přístav 18600
A haven of peace

In 1822, Prague's first commercial harbour was built in Karlín. For about 100 years the ships that sailed to Hamburg via the Vltava and Elbe were loaded and unloaded there. Later the course of the river was moved, and the harbour gradually lost its importance. The district of Karlín continued to exist, bordered on one side by the river, but there was no place here for people to play by the water with children, or simply to chill out.

In 2014, three young fathers who had moved to the area took the initiative and created a spot by themselves. The city authorities put a small patch of ground between the river and the bike path at their disposal free of charge. Here they cleaned up the rubbish that had been dumped, built a bar – and Přístav was complete. The name means harbour, and 18600 is the postcode.

Don't expect any well-organised luxury. A short distance from the riverbank stands a shipping container with a white tarpaulin where you can buy coffee, beer or a sausage that you can cook yourself on a camp fire, or on one of the barbecues that are for hire. The facilities are above all functional and cheap – the seats are concrete tables. Children can play on climbing frames made from concrete rings, swings made from car tyres or hammocks. Occasionally cultural events such as concerts or discussions are held here. There's a space for beach volleyball, and a washroom.

Harbour 18600 has become a place where you can get away from the city bustle for a short time – even though, just a few metres away, stand the huge office blocks that have sprung up like mushrooms in Karlín in recent years, and given an official character to what used to be a working-class district. The lease of the land by the city authorities is only valid for a transitional period. Let's hope that Harbour 18600 doesn't meet the same fate as its much larger predecessor.

Address Rohanský ostrov, 186 00 Prague 8, www.18600.cz | Getting there Metro B to Křižíkova, then go along Thámova and U Mlýnského kanálu, finally crossing the bike path to the river | Hours Bar: May–Sept, daily noon–11pm | Tip Main Point at Pobřežní 21 was voted the best office building in the world in 2011. On the first floor is a gallery with an art collection – investment assets of the Kooperativa insurance company. Works by Jan Zrzavý, Mikoláš Aleš and other Czech artists can be viewed free, Tue & Thur 10am–6pm.

76_ The Research Centre
A free mini zoo in the middle of the city

So, you've done your shopping in the Nový Smíchov mall in Anděl, and now you want to relax in green surroundings? No problem. Go to the first floor of the shopping centre, head towards the toilets and take the glass door leading outside. A walkway takes you to Sacré Coeur Park. If you turn right, you reach a green gate behind which two small inquisitive kangaroos will be looking out for you.

The research centre in Smíchov is mainly an educational facility for children, but it is also a small zoo in the city centre.

The lush garden full of trees is home to more than 100 kinds of animal. Past the aviaries and open-air compounds you can have a wonderful walk, seeing kangaroos, ponies, llamas, goats, ostriches and parrots. In the herb garden, the scents change with every step you take. Don't forget to look inside the strange little house with compartments full of twigs, blades of grass – and chunks of porous concrete. This is an "insect hotel," which various species use to get through the winter.

The research centre also breeds crocodiles and other reptiles, monkeys and exotic plants. You will find them in the tropical terrarium and the hothouse, which can be visited on certain days for a very modest fee. Plants and small pets are on sale, and courses in gardening are on offer.

Children can amuse themselves for hours here, and adults can restore their energy in a green environment. But before you leave, take a look at the map to be on the safe side. Apart from the route described above, there are two further entrances and exits – a small path between the fence of the clinic and the sports centre in Drtinova, and the blue gate next to the house at Holečkova 29. In contrast to Prague's zoo, for which advertising is displayed on every corner, the research centre's garden is a hidden oasis of peace, and it's well worth making the effort to find it.

Address Stanice přírodovědců DDM hl. M. Prahy, Drtinova 1a, 150 00 Prague 5, www.ddmpraha.cz/stanice-prirodovedcu | **Getting there** Metro B to Anděl; tram 9, 12, 15, 20 to Arbesovo náměstí; bus 176 to Kobrova (entrance via Holečkova 29) | **Hours** Garden: Mon–Fri 9am–7pm, Sat & Sun 10am–4pm (Nov–Mar closed at weekends), terrarium and hothouse Tue 2–6pm, Wed 9am–noon and 2–4pm, Thu 2–4pm | **Tip** Further up Holečkova is what used to be a convent. The Neo-Romanesque Church of St Gabriel, famous for its mysterious art of the Beuron School, is still used for celebrating Mass. The many-towered building on its left is used by the postal service.

77 Rikatádo

Take me home, country roads

"Tramping" is a typically Czech phenomenon:, trips into the countryside with no fixed aim, passionate and free. The interwar period was the time when the movement began to found tramp settlements with names like Ascalona, and romantic songs were sung around flickering camp fires. In the 1980s the feeling of taking part in a conspiracy against the regime contributed to these idealised visions of the Wild West. This explains – at least in part – why tramping reached its peak at that time. Every Friday, tramps with hats, rucksacks and guitars headed for the train stations of Prague, and played country songs in the evenings. For fans of this culture, there is no finer venue in Prague than the Palmovka music club, better known under its old name, Rikatádo.

As soon as you get to the entrance, you breathe the atmosphere of the Wild West: above the stairs hang pictures of saloons and prairies, the walls are clad in light-coloured wood, and a swinging door leads to the toilets. At the bar you can take your place in one of two horse saddles to knock back your whiskey. All the seats at the bar used to look like this, but as the clientele changed, most of the saddles were replaced with classic bar stools.

In recent years the club has evolved. When it was founded in the 1990s, nothing but country music and suchlike genres was played, every evening. Now rock, reggae and big beat are also on the programme, and the original country sound can only be heard once a week. Occasionally the management succeeds in tempting legendary bands like Fešáci to the club – but they can't make time stand still. Most of the famous Czech country musicians are around 65 years old, and their fans are in a similar age group. However, tramps are tough, so there's no doubt that you'll be able to come here for a weekly dose of old-fashioned rhythms for a few years yet.

Address Pod Hájkem 1 (entrance from Na Žertvách), 180 00 Prague 8, www.hudebniklub.cz | **Getting there** Metro B to Palmovka, then go along Na Žertvách | **Hours** Sun–Fri 11am–2am, Sat 4pm–2am (sometimes later) | **Tip** Behind the bus station at the other end of Na Žertvách is a synagogue dating from 1858. It's worth a visit, but is only open occasionally for cultural and religious events. It's a reminder that Libeň was the second-biggest Jewish settlement in the Prague area.

78﹈Rothmayer's Villa

In the footsteps of Josef Sudek

Without its garden, the villa of the architect Otto Rothmayer would be unimaginable. Rothmayer's friend Josef Sudek was fascinated by what he called its "little enchanted garden" and it was here that he created his famous photographic still lifes with trees, tree stumps and white chairs. Many years later, the spell still works. Although it's not especially big, it has many romantic, intimate corners. Rothmayer's son sold the house and garden to the city of Prague, which renovated it and opened it to the public in 2015.

Rothmayer worked closely with the Slovenian architect Josip Plečnik, who was asked by President Tomáš Garrigue Masaryk to restore Prague's decaying castle. When Plečnik returned to Ljubljana in 1921, with the work half-completed, Rothmayer took over Plečnik's duties, and before long he was working more or less independently on the renovation of the castle.

When he designed his family villa in 1929, he took inspiration from Plečnik's project, conceiving the cube-shaped house, with its cylindrical addition for the staircase, as a country house in the middle of fields.

Today the villa no longer stands in countryside, but is surrounded by other buildings. Nevertheless the interior fittings retain the simple country-house style. The kitchen, the main room, smells of wood. Rothmayer came from a family of carpenters, and so made most of his own furniture. The stove and the books are also part of the original furnishings; as a visitor you feel that its previous residents are still living here.

One feature of the house has disappeared, however. Rothmayer was a passionate collector of vases, miniature bottles and small pictures, which filled every last corner of his rooms. Sudek liked to photograph these, too, but hardly any of them remain. In the garden, by contrast, everything is just as it used to be – including the picture-perfect elements.

Address U Páté baterie 896/50, 160 00 Prague 6 | **Getting there** Tram 1, 2 to Vojenská nemocnice | **Hours** Tours: Tue, Thu, Sat, Sun 10am, noon, 2pm & 4pm; must be booked in advance at www.muzeumprahy.cz/rothmayerova-vila | **Tip** To get an impression of the luxury of the interwar years, visit the nearby Villa Müller at Nad Hradním vodojemem 14/642. This fine residence of a construction magnate was designed by one of the great architects of the time, Adolf Loos.

79   The Savings Bank

All that glitters really is gold

Grey and boring: that would be a reasonable description of most of the public buildings in the Czech Republic. But there are some exceptions, for example the branch of the Czech Savings Bank in Rytířská. From the outside it's not especially striking – a fine building, but it doesn't stand out amongst the other palaces of Prague. Inside, however, you are greeted by a marble staircase that leads up to a splendid lobby in the Neo-Renaissance style, filled with paintings, statues and gilded objects – the result of the wealth of the late 19th century combined with the endeavours of that era to support Czech arts.

The building, which opened in 1894, was designed as the seat of the Prague savings bank. This entirely Czech bank was founded in 1875; the first person to invest his savings was none other than the famous "Father of the Nation", František Palacký. The savings account with the number 1,000,001 is said to have belonged to Tomáš Garrigue Masaryk. The opulent decoration of the bank was the work of the painter Mikoláš Aleš and the sculptor Bohuslav Schnirch.

In the 1950s this exclusive circle was joined, paradoxically, by the communist president Klement Gottwald, when the building was made into a museum. The combination of architectural opulence with an exhibition about the history of the Communist Party, mainly visited by bored school kids, must have made for a Kafkaesque experience.

In the course of privatisation, the savings bank got its building back in 1989. Today the lobby is a normal branch of the bank, and open to the public during business hours. But don't be surprised if the security staff keep a close eye on you – and don't forget that taking photographs is prohibited. However, the issue here is whether the scene might not be too much for your camera. Because the saying "All that glitters is not gold" definitely doesn't apply here.

Address Česká Spořitelna, Rytířská 29, 110 00 Prague 1 | **Getting there** Metro A, B to Můstek | **Hours** Mon–Fri 9am–6pm | **Tip** The name of the small, tourist-free lane V Kotcích opposite the savings bank refers to the little shops – *kotce* – in which clothmakers, linen merchants and other textile traders sold their wares from the 14th century onwards. In the 19th century they were converted into housing, while others were demolished for the construction of the savings bank.

80 The Secret Passage

A perfectly hidden café

At Spálená 15 you will find a narrow, dirty entrance, covered in spray paint. Unless you're a student at the nearby High School for Publicity Studies, it's unlikely that you'd think of entering it. But be bold, and go in. Not only is it a considerable shortcut between Spálená and Opatovická, it's also a place where two surprises await you.

First of all, the passage leads to a small courtyard, partially covered with a glass roof, and from there into a larger yard. Here is the first surprise: the minimalist café Super Tramp Coffee, whose name supposedly comes from a remark that only a "supertramp" would discover it.

You can enjoy their delicious coffee at a table outside, while looking at the inner façade of the building and the extensive terrace, which seems so perfectly dilapidated and neglected that you could certainly set a romantic film on the site.

But that's not all. The second surprise is that you're looking at the houses in which the first Czech translations were made of the works of Karl May, the German author of tales of the Wild West. Both buildings, connected by a passageway, and later the adjoining house on the corner in Opatovická, belonged to the Vilímek family. In the late 19th and first half of the 20th century this family owned one of the best-known publishers in the country, the first to use a rotating printing press, in 1891. Apart from the works of Karl May, they also printed books by Jules Verne and the Sherlock Holmes stories.

In the 1990s a scandalous privatisation of the buildings took place, and today, apart from the high school, only a few companies are based here. The buildings await renovation, seemingly in vain. So when you leave the courtyard and enter Opatovická, you'll find an unwelcoming, graffiti-covered entrance on that side too. Perhaps that's a good thing: secret passages need perfect camouflage.

Address Spálená 15 and Opatovická 18, 110 00 Prague 1 | **Getting there** Metro B to Národní třída | **Hours** Super Tramp Coffee: Mon – Fri 8am – 8pm, see www.facebook.com/supertrampcoffee.cz | **Tip** An easily overlooked plaque on the nearby Church of St Michael commemorates a famous visitor: in 1923 and 1928 the doctor and Nobel Prize laureate Albert Schweitzer gave organ concerts here.

81 The Secret Playground
Children in Wonderland

Children and sightseeing – now that's quite a topic. There's a constant need to come up with good ideas for kids. Perhaps the best approach is to tempt them by suggesting a mysterious destination – like the secret playground in the Nový Svět (New World) district, which is only a few steps away from Hradčany castle.

Of course the playground isn't really secret, but it is concealed behind a high wall, and it's easy to overlook the little gate through which you enter. On the other side, the long space is bordered by a wire-mesh fence, designed to stop children from getting into the adjoining moat. The playground is surprisingly well equipped. It's been renovated twice in the last ten years, the first time on the initiative of Livia Klausová, the former Czech first lady, who inaugurated it in 2009. Today kids can clamber about on modern climbing frames and whizz down the slides, while grown-ups enjoy a bit of peace and quiet – though the "quiet" is relative, of course, as the playground is popular with local residents. Tourists, however, seldom find their way here.

The whole of the Nový Svět district is like this, by the way. Although its narrow, crooked lanes are only a stone's throw from the castle, not many visitors to the city make the detour to come here. And yet it's one of the most picturesque quarters in Prague. In the 1920s it was still a poor area, but it has evolved over the decades into an artists' quarter. If you're lucky you might encounter the surrealist film maker Jan Švankmajer, who lives in one of the little houses in the district.

On the way home, a little imagination and storytelling might be required if your children want to know why the house at the corner of Černínská and Nový Svět doesn't have an entrance of its own, but still possesses a number. Perhaps Švankmajer's Alice lives in the building – you never know!

Address Nový Svět, 118 00 Prague 1 (the playground entrance is opposite no. 11) |
Getting there Tram 22 to Pohořelec, then go towards the castle, past the Maria Loreto
pilgrimage site, then along Černínská and right into the lane called Nový Svět. The route
from Brusnice tram stop along U Brusnice is shorter but less attractive. | **Tip** Only a few
metres from the playground entrance, a plaque on one of the houses tells us that the famous
Danish astronomer Tycho de Brahe died near here. But this information is incorrect:
he actually died in a house that once stood on the site of today's Jan Kepler School in
Parléřova, near the Pohořelec tram stop.

82 The Semmering Railway
Romantic rail tracks in Prague

When the tramlines on Plzeňská ulice were renewed in 2010, the Prague transport authority proposed diverting the trams to a section of rails that had previously been little used. In its early days of operation, passengers ran to and fro, from one window to another, so that they could enjoy the overwhelming view. And no wonder! The "Prague Semmering" is one of the most attractive railway routes – not just in Prague, but anywhere.

The best way to get to know it is to take a round trip, at the weekend, on the *vláček motoráček*, a historic train built in the 1950s. The breathtaking route starts at the central station and passes through a variety of scenery. You can look forward to a tunnel more than a kilometre long, a section on raised tracks through Nusle, a view of Prague castle and the Vyšehrad from the railway bridge that crosses the Vltava, two viaducts spanning the beautiful Prokop valley, and majestic cliffs. Furthermore, you'll go past districts of fine houses and glass office buildings, plus long stretches of woodland that will make you forget you're in a major city. The ride terminates at the station in Praha-Zličín. You can either return by the same route – all you have to do is to stay seated on the train – or walk to the tram, which takes you back to the city centre from a nearby stop.

Prague's Semmering railway owes its name to a most extreme example of a complicated train route – the Semmering railway in Austria. If you're not able to ride the Prague version (which covers an altitude varying by 93 metres) at the weekend, then no matter: on weekdays the S 65 train runs at intervals of approximately an hour. However, in this case the journey begins and ends in Smíchov, and you're not treated to the crossing of the Vltava. And the windows of this train can't be opened and closed in charming fashion by turning a handle.

Address Praha hlavní nádraží, Wilsonova 300/8, 110 00 Prague 1 | **Getting there** Metro C to Hlavní nádraží | **Hours** See timetable at www.kzc.cz/vlak/prazsky-motoracek; click on "Jízdní řád" on the right; for both legs of the journey you only need the normal 90-minute ticket for Prague public transport | **Tip** You also get a fine view of the rocky Prokop valley on the 15 minute trip with the S 6 train line from Smíchovské nádraží to Praha-Řeporyje.

83__The Sewage Works
Plain abseiling!

Do you remember the opening scene of *Mission Impossible IV*, where Tom Cruise escapes from a Russian jail? Well, if you want to feel like this fearless hero, at least for one magnificent moment, you don't have to go to Moscow. Cruise's escape through a sewer was filmed in Prague – in the sewage works in Bubeneč. But don't think stinking tunnels: this Art Nouveau building, with its conspicuous chimneys and subterranean labyrinth, is a genuine sightseeing tip.

In the 19th century, Prague's sewage still flowed into the Vltava. Then the British civil engineer William H. Lindley was entrusted with the mission of designing a new system of sewers. The project was so modern that the city showed it off to foreign visitors. Altogether, Lindley built 100 kilometres of sewers. These drained waste water along gradients by gravity alone, even from low-lying districts of the city. As a precaution against floods, the sewers were built on two levels. The network was completed in 1906 with the construction of sewage works in Bubeneč.

Thanks to its appearance, and at the same time its thankless task, the building got the nickname "stinking Karlštejn." Into it 120 million litres of waste water flowed daily, initially through a grid that filtered out the worst of its contents. After this the water passed into sand filters and finally into a sludge tank, where pumps powered by steam engines extracted more of the waste matter – up to 30 wagons of it per day.

The building was in operation until 1967. Today it's a museum in which the sewers, tanks and machines made by Breitfeld & Daněk – still functioning – can be admired. They look as if they've come straight from a novel by Jules Verne. Bolder visitors are helped by the museum guides to climb up the ventilation chimney and abseil down to the inside of the sewage plant. Tom Cruise could do that in his sleep. What about you?

Address Muzeum Stará Čistírna, Papírenská 6, 160 00 Prague 6, stara-cistirna.cz |
Getting there Metro A to Hradčanská, then bus 131 to Goetheho and go under the
railway bridge to Papírenská | **Hours** Tours: Mon – Fri 11am & 2pm, Sat, Sun and holidays
10am, 11.30am, 1pm, 3pm & 4.30pm | **Tip** Have a beer afterwards at Na Slamníku
(Wolkerova 566/12), a cult pub that made its name with alternative rock concerts. Today
you're more likely to meet diplomats from the nearby Russian embassy than rockers.

84 __ Sir Winton's Platform

Saved from the hell of Auschwitz

On 31 July, 1939, when she boarded a train to London with her sister at Prague's central station, Hana Kleinerová was just twelve years old. Their parents waved to the girls and promised that they would be reunited soon. This never happened, as both parents died in Auschwitz. On Platform 1 there is a small monument dedicated to the fate of these two girls and the other children who were saved shortly before World War II, thanks to the foresight of their parents and the young British broker Nicholas Winton. The story of how he organised the transport by rail of Czech children to British foster families is well known today. Yet for 50 years almost no one knew about it.

Even his wife Greta learned about it only by chance, when she found a suitcase containing a list of Jewish names in the attic. She passed the documents to the historian Elisabeth Maxwell, who invited Winton to take part in a BBC broadcast in 1988. Here he described in public for the first time how he'd planned to go skiing in Switzerland, but cancelled the holiday at the last minute at the request of friends. Instead he travelled to Prague to help a humanitarian organisation carry out the evacuation of Jews and others persecuted by the Nazis. He focussed on children, looked for British families to adopt them and handled the bureaucratic formalities. A total of eight trains carrying 669 children, most of them Jewish, made the journey from Prague to London.

When, at the end of the BBC programme, the men and women whom he had saved stood up around him, it was a highly emotional moment. Sir Nicholas Winton deservedly became a hero overnight; since 2009 a bronze statue of him and two of his "children" has stood in the Central Station. It is dedicated to those who were saved, and to the 15,131 Czech and Slovak children who died in concentration camps.

Address Central Station, platform 1, Wilsonova 300/8, 110 00 Prague 1 | **Getting there** Metro C to Hlavní nádraží | **Tip** The bronze statue stands directly in front of the government saloon, a beautiful Art Nouveau waiting room that was built for famous passengers, and can now be hired for events. It is open to the public each autumn for European Cultural Heritage Day.

85 __ Smíchov
Witnesses to bygone days

Country houses with agricultural outbuildings, surrounded by fields and orchards: these estates were built by wealthy citizens close to the city walls, in an area that was dominated by farming for centuries. In some places they are a unique reminder of times past, but elsewhere a monument to ignorance of history and heritage. If you take a walk through Smíchov, you can discover both. You'll need a street map and good shoes.

Cibulka, for example, welcomes you with walled-up windows and a roof that has been patched up with plastic sheeting. At its imposing gate, a security firm's sign deters visitors – perhaps to prevent the return of squatters, who at least did something to maintain the building. Continue past the Chinese Pavilion into Plzeňská, then turn right in Zahradníčkova. After that go diagonally to the left until the path takes you up the hill to the estate called Kotlářka. It presents a more cheerful picture: following many years of arbitrary communist rule, this house is being repaired by those who inherited it. They're running a guesthouse and a restaurant, which both offer sensationally good value for money. From here go down the main street and into U Kotlářky, at the end of which you walk up steeply through the woods, then go left across the field and finally right past the sports ground. On the right, in the undergrowth, is the dilapidated Skalka estate. Though in the case of Cibulka you can still pretend, here it's plain to see that the owners are just waiting for this protected heritage building to collapse so that they can make a profit by building new apartments.

To raise your spirits again, you can admire the attractively renovated remains of the Klikovka estate in the street of the same name. Or in Na Hřebenkách, visit the little-known park by Dolní Palata, which was converted into an institute for the visually handicapped in 1893.

Address Cibulka 118, 150 00 Prague 5, further information about the estates in Smíchov at smichov.blog.cz | **Getting there** Metro B to Anděl, then tram 9, 10, 15, 16, 21 to Kavalírka, then bus 123 to U lesíka, and finally through the park and to the left of the viewing tower | **Tip** You can see more recent architecture in Švédská, where there are magnificent detached houses from the first third of the 20th century. Then cross Holečkova ulice and admire the view of Prague from the viewing tower in Sacré Coeur Park. Cross the bridge to the shopping centre and walk through it to Anděl.

86__Sputnik

A whetstone for children's trousers

The climbing frame that the artist Zdeněk Němeček made in 1960, modelled on the Soviet Sputnik satellite, exudes 100 per cent nostalgia. In Stromovka Park thousands of children climbed up a ladder to the giant sphere and slid back down. When the slide became so worn down that only a concrete surface remained, it quickly got its nickname: "the whetstone for children's trousers."

Aesthetes from abroad have declared the five-tonne sculpture in the "Brussels style" to be art. A life-size photograph of it even hung in New York's MoMA. But the Sputnik was neglected in its own country. When it became dilapidated, the authorities put bars across the entrance, though that didn't stop one small boy from putting his head between them – and it took the assistance of firemen to put an end to his adventure. This led to a proposal to remove the climbing frame altogether, but at the eleventh hour the Sputnik was saved by Rudolf Břínek, an art collector, who installed it in his garden in Dejvice. Here you can peer at it through the fence – and it looks as good as new.

The best thing about moving the Sputnik was that it's now in select company: this is where the Modernist Baba estate was built in 1932. The villas were tailor-made for Prague's high society by renowned architects, including Josef Gočár – or perhaps his pupils. Although several houses were later reconstructed in an insensitive way, Baba is nevertheless one of the best-preserved Modernist estates in Europe.

In the streets Na Ostrohu, Průhledová, Na Babě and Nad Paťankou are 33 detached houses with flat roofs and terraces. They're arranged in a chequerboard pattern, so as not to spoil the view of Prague from any of them. It's an irony of fate that Baba is admired by few people other than students of architecture. As with the Sputnik, the Czechs seem to have forgotten this special district of the city.

Address Na Babě 1779/9, 160 00 Prague 6 | **Getting there** Metro A to Hradčanská, then bus 131 to U Matěje | **Tip** At the end of Nad Paťankou, go to the right across the field to the ruins of the Baba summer lodge and look across to the opposite bank of the Vltava, preferably with binoculars. If you're in luck, you'll see giraffes, antelopes and ostriches – you have a view of Prague Zoo.

87 __ St Adalbert

100 temporary years

You can't miss this church in Zenklova, one of the main streets in Libeň. The building, with its white walls and dark wooden tower resembling a spiked helmet, seems as if it wants to swallow people up. It would fit into a fantasy film better than a modern capital city. And in fact its history has a touch of the fantastic: the church should have disappeared from here a long time ago.

In the late 19th century the population of this district expanded rapidly, and the Catholic believers of Libeň could no longer all crowd into their little palace chapel. And so in 1904 they leased a plot of land in Thomayerovy sady and began to collect money to build a large church. They planned to start construction in ten years' time. They were assisted by the Catholic Bonifác association, which provided funds to build a smaller place of worship in the meantime. St Adalbert was consecrated in 1905.

For this temporary solution, the architect Emil Králíček opted for wood as his principal building material. If you look up at the ceiling, you'll see a complicated system of crossbeams with leaf decoration; the wooden wall between the nave and the sacristy, which has an air of folklore about it, has similar adornments. The dormer windows in the roof are fixed partly to the wooden wall and partly to the masonry.

The fact that we can still enjoy the sight of this church today is mainly due to lack of funds. For a long time the congregation couldn't raise enough money to build a larger place of worship. Then there were delays in getting approval for the plans, until finally the whole campaign ground to a halt. That's why this example of early Art Nouveau religious architecture is still standing; it may be the only temporary building in the Czech Republic with protected heritage status. Now that the number of churchgoers has fallen significantly, its capacity exceeds the demand.

Address Kostel sv. Vojtěcha, U Meteoru 599, 180 00 Prague 8 | **Getting there** Metro B to Palmovka, then on foot or by tram 3, 10, 24 to Stejskalova | **Hours** Mass: Tue, Sat 5pm, Sun 10am & 2.30pm | **Tip** Next to the church is another Art Nouveau gem by Emil Králíček: the famous Sokol Building, a gymnasium. If you glance inside you will see an imposing marble staircase with brass lamps and a geometric balustrade, unusual in a sports hall.

88 _ The Station Pub

Where democracy drinks

Bohumil Hrabal once described a French prime minister's admiration for Czech democracy as he saw it in the make-up of customers in the U Zlatého tygra pub, where you would find barbers and decorators alongside judges and politicians. Unfortunately this famous tavern in the Old Town has become a little too well known today.

So if you'd like to experience some pub democracy without reserving a table, pay a visit to the Dejvické Nádraží station restaurant, generally known simply as Nádražka. Where else do so many people from all walks of life come together, other than at a railway station? As well as passengers waiting for a train, you'll see older regulars, students, fans of the Sparta Prague football club, business people drinking beer after work, young women looking at their tablets and men reading books.

In the beer garden you can sit beneath stately chestnut trees; a few small tables stand right on the covered train platform. In the station building, which dates from 1871, unconventional bands occasionally perform. The rooms, with their high Neo-Renaissance ceilings, are decorated in a kind of art-punk surrealism, with the conspicuous face of the legendary television presenter Miloš Frýba. His earnest, all-seeing smile looks down on everyone who truly takes alcohol seriously.

You can eat here, or drink coloured water costing 8Kč – but the low prices for drinks of a completely different kind are the main attraction. Shots cost from 10Kč upwards, and the pricing policy for beer is similarly customer-friendly. Its quality may be debatable, but it's better not to start a discussion on the subject with the head waiter. He is not the personification of kindness – quite fittingly for a pub of this kind.

It seems almost ironic that, on the platform opposite, there is usually a silver train with an interactive anti-drugs exhibition for children.

Address Restaurace Dejvické Nádraží, Václavkova 1, 160 00 Prague 6, www.nadrazka.cz | **Getting there** Metro A to Hradčanská, then walk a short distance along Dejvická and Václavkova | **Hours** Daily 9am–midnight | **Tip** If you'd like to see another authentic place like this, get on a train, and nine minutes later you'll reach Masarykovo nádraží, where Bistro Flip awaits you at the tram stop. It's open from 7am to 8pm and only sells bottled beer. If you want to sit at one of the dirty tables, you pay 2Kč extra. Only for those who like extreme experiences.

89 __ Stínadla

The mysterious Vonts

Church towers, dark courtyards and winding lanes where gas lamps cast sharp shadows after dusk: this is the Prague district of Stínadla, which is ruled by a boy gang, the Vonts. Every evening the Vonts, aka "Rapid Arrows," make their way there to have adventures. Whole generations of Czech youngsters have grown up with these five boys, devouring the children's books by cult author Jaroslav Foglar. The author has never revealed the location of this fictitious quarter of the city. But it's probable that he took inspiration from the area around St Agnes Monastery and the Church of St Kastulus, which has been called Na Františku since time immemorial.

Once a poor district on the edge of the city, full of dark little houses, taverns and brothels, this area around the streets Řásnovka, U Milosrdných and Kozí has kept its special atmosphere to this day. You meet few people in its narrow alleys. Between the newly painted façades, a wall of bricks or a wooden gate peeps through here and there, as in Foglar's novels.

In 2007 one of the lanes was officially given the name Ve Stínadlech, but the red street sign is often carried off as a trophy by dedicated fans of Foglar. In fact Ve Stínadlech is not much more than a narrow passage between the wall of the priest's house and a fence. After dark,this is a gloomy spot, but in the blocked-up window at the end of the alley there shines a drawing of a yellow pin, the sign by which the Vonts are recognised. Occasionally the wall has a drawing of the "Hedgehog in the Cage," a famous puzzle that has actually found its way out of the books and into souvenir shops.

If you don't see any scraps of paper with coded messages sticking to the wall, don't be surprised: the Vonts are arranging their next meeting at this very moment. Stínadla may be a world of fiction, but the myth of the Rapid Arrows lives on here.

Address Ve Stínadlech, 110 00 Prague 1 | **Getting there** Tram 6, 8, 15, 26 to Dlouhá, then along Dlouhá and Rybná towards Haštalské náměstí | **Tip** If you want some excellent fast food, you'll find the best fish and chips in Prague at the bistro Fish & Chips 21 Dlouha St. (Dlouhá 21).

90 __ 90 Strahov Stadium

A concrete monstrosity above the city

Put your hand on your heart: are you a bit of a megalomaniac? No? Really? Not even a tiny bit? That's a shame. Then the Strahov Stadium is probably not for you.

This is the world's biggest stadium. Covering an area of 202 by 310 metres – equivalent to nine football pitches – with a capacity for 220,000 spectators, it makes the Nou Camp in Barcelona, which "only" holds 100,000, seem pretty small.

If you like imagining a lot of athletes all doing the same thing at the same time, then the Strahov Stadium is just what you're looking for: members of the patriotic gymnasts' movement Sokol used to spend their time here doing synchronised hoop gymnastics and knee bends, or throwing balls. Later, the communists perfected mass gymnastics to the point of absurdity: during the so-called *Spartakiads*, children were let out early for their summer holidays so that the city could prepare to be inundated by gymnasts from all parts of the country. In 1985, at the last *Spartakiad*, around 190,000 gymnasts went through their drill in front of 1.2 million spectators. And that wasn't even a record.

After 1989 the popularity of collective exertion declined; the Strahov Stadium was then used for big concerts. A thought-provoking event in 1990 was the first concert in Prague by the Rolling Stones, before which President Václav Havel addressed the audience of 100,000.

Today most of the facilities are used as a training ground by the football club Sparta Praha. Although the stadium precinct also houses an indoor swimming pool, a Vietnamese bistro and a car repair shop, most of the stands are crumbling. This is hardly a tragedy, as only the 1930s brick sections are of architectural interest, but as a protected monument the stadium can't be demolished. So you'll be able to admire the reinforced concrete of the east stand for a while yet – if you have a soft spot for megalomania.

Address Vaníčkova, Atletická and Zátopkova ulice, 160 17 Prague 6 | **Getting there** Take the Petřín funicular, then walk past the observatory and student hall of residence or take bus 143 (from Dejvická) or 176 (from Karlovo náměstí) | **Hours** Most areas are closed to the public | **Tip** Two small tram stations are reminders of the old glory days of mass gymnastics. The platforms, dilapidated and covered with grass, are below the Strahov hill at the end of Bělohorská, opposite the Hotel Pyramida.

91 The Street Light

Cubist art at Jungmannovo náměstí

You'll find it on the covers of books about design and architecture, but you may not have seen it in real life. Yet if you live in Prague, you're sure to have walked past it a few times. An icon of Czech Cubism, the street light by Emil Králíček is hidden in a corner of Jungmannovo náměstí square, near the entrance to the garden of the Church of Our Lady of the Snows.

Its existence is largely fortuitous. In 1912 and 1913 the architect Králíček was designing the pharmacy on Wenceslas Square. He also had the task of restoring the rear side of the building on Jungmannovo náměstí and everything around it. He rebuilt the old garden wall and the gate with the stone relief of the Virgin Mary, and created flower beds, which unfortunately no longer survive, on the pavement. And above all, he made this dark, unwelcoming corner shine again, by means of a Cubist street light. At first it was a flop. The press wrote scornfully that the light was only advertising the nearby U Pinkasů pub, as the column's piled-up pyramidal bases of artificial stone were reminiscent of beer barrels.

In the 1990s the small stone bench at the foot of the column still stank of urine and rubbish. Today, by contrast, everything around the street lamp is clean and tidy. As a precaution, however, the glass and metal lamp at the top has been replaced by a copy, and the original stored in the National Gallery of Prague.

The street light is now a well-established art object. Though street furniture is often reduced to the qualities of functionality and robustness, the Cubist lamp shows how far items that seem inconspicuous can put their stamp on the whole appearance of a city. This is one reason why urban furnishings are often the work of leading architects and designers today. In this respect the street lamp was ahead of its time, and is a fine example of the shining power of true art.

Address Jungmannovo náměstí, 110 00 Prague 1 | Getting there Metro B to Můstek, then take the exit to Jungmannovo náměstí | Tip In summer the sign next to the gate behind the street lamp draws visitors to the beer garden of the U Pinkasů pub. This long, narrow outdoor space, bounded by the wall of a house on one side, and the massive Church of Our Lady of the Snows on the other, will amaze you, as it truly resembles the yard of a medieval tavern.

92 Strudel

The sweet smell of success

From the top down to the basement: you could characterise Petr Šusta's career in these words. But wait a minute. This is not a tale of financial downfall. On the contrary – it's a success story that smells of cinnamon and grated apples.

Petr Šusta used to work in the TV tower in Žižkov, but in 1993, when times were getting hard after the end of communism, he set up a bakery for traditional Bohemian strudel, using the room reserved for parking children's buggies in the concrete residential block where he lived. Instead of the usual flaky pastry he used strudel dough, stretched paper thin, and lovingly filled it with fresh apples, curd cheese, poppy seeds and *zwetschge* plums.

For more than 20 years his strudel has been extremely popular, not only among the gourmets of Prague but also, thanks to reports on CNN, much further afield. This is paradoxical, as many locals don't know his shop. The entrance is concealed between doors to buildings, and only a laconic sign reading *ŠTRÚDL* draws attention to it.

The block of flats, by the way, is a result of the so-called redevelopment of the district of Žižkov. In the 1980s communist urban planners wanted to tear down most of this picturesque quarter and replace it with a concrete estate. Fortunately only the first phase was carried out.

The residents resisted, and a group of architects calculated that it would actually be cheaper to restore the houses. The planners' response was that renovation on this scale was not possible in a socialist society, as too few skilled workers were available. Small businesses had been nationalised just like large companies – and artisans were thus few and far between. This led to the contradictory situation that a successful small business was established in, of all places, a building that was constructed because the socialist regime was opposed to small private enterprises.

Address Jeseniova 909/29, 130 00 Prague 3, www.strudl-zizkov.cz | **Getting there** Metro A to Flora, then bus 136 or 175 to Rokycanova, and a five-minute walk | **Hours** Mon–Fri 8am–noon & 1–5pm | **Tip** Apart from delaying demolition, the opponents of redevelopment had a further triumph: saving an old school in Neo-Renaissance style, that now stands proudly between buildings of prefabricated concrete on nearby Komenského náměstí.

93 _ The Terezka Fountain
Almost the world's richest statue

"You sit by the silver spring, Terezka, in the niche/ Oh, maiden of stone, I give you my love." With these words Petr Rezek, now a largely forgotten poet, sang the praises of the stone statue. The fountain with the figure of a young girl, called Terezka by the people of Prague, almost had a romance of this kind. A legend tells that an old soldier who lived nearby fell in love with the statue, and actually left it 10,000 guilders in his will. Nevertheless, Terezka did not become the richest statue in the world, as the soldier's family prevented the bequest.

Her tender features, dreamy expression and physical charms make Terezka one of the loveliest statues in the city. Yet she sits inconspicuously on the outer wall of the Clam-Gallas Palace on Mariánské náměstí. She was made from sandstone by Václav Prachner in the first half of the 19th century. At that time the houses here had no running water, so women came every day with tin cups to scoop the water into barrels that they took home on their backs.

It is not known why the fountain is called Terezka, though It's said to have been nicknamed by the women who came for water. Some say it was named after one of them. Yet another version states that the girl who modelled for the figure was called Terezka. In fact the statue is an allegory of the river Vltava: from the jug in Terezka's right hand a jet of water trickles into the basin, while the stone-carved stream flowing from her other hand is decorated with five stars. The stars are the symbol of St John Nepomuk, who died a martyr's death in the Vltava.

As a result of weathering, but also because everyone wanted to touch it, the statue began to deteriorate, so the damaged original was taken to the National Gallery in 1953. Today we see a copy, but this in no way diminishes Terezka's beauty. After gazing at her, you may want to change your will.

Address Mariánské náměstí, 110 00 Prague 1 | Getting there Metro A or tram 2, 17, 18 to Staroměstská | Tip Walk along Linhartská to the New City Hall if you want to honour the memory of Josef Kajetán Tyl, who wrote the words of the Czech national anthem. However, you'll have to tilt your head back, as the plaque commemorating Tyl's period of residence here from 1840 to 1843 is high up, on the third floor.

94 Three "Fours" Crawl

Pubs, the way they used to be

In the late 1980s the legendary underground band Psí vojáci sang a song about a dirty pub on the edge of the city. Almost 30 years on, you can still enjoy this rough-and-ready pub culture – and you don't even have to go that far. In the city centre several beer bars have survived that were assigned under the old regime to "Price Category IV" – the lowest classification.

Start your pub crawl at U Žaludů. It's worth coming here just to see the streets Na Zbořenci and Na Zderaze, as both of them are on a slope, which creates some picturesque corners; even during rush hour you won't come across many people here. In the pub you will then find everything that can be expected of a proper "Category Four": cheap beer, regulars with lots of character, brusque but efficient service, and prices that nowadays are only normal in pubs far away from Prague.

The surroundings of the second stop on the tour are definitely not to be recommended – the sole highlight in Charvátova is the U Jelínků bar itself. Some might maintain that this pub is not a true "Four," since it is an old-established Prague tavern that the writer Jaroslav Hašek was fond of. It differs from the two others in the quality of the beer. The Pilsner Urquell here is quite simply in a class of its own. What gives its two small rooms a "Four" rating – however inexact the definition may be today – are the low prices, the almost complete absence of tourists, and the feeling that time has stood still here. The landlord's majestic moustache, and his skill at pouring the beer, are essential elements of the place.

The scene is similar in U Rotundy – including another highly professional landlord. The dirt is now a thing of the past. But do be prepared to put your clothes in the washing machine as soon as you get home – at least until the Czech Republic gets round to banning smoking in pubs.

Address U Žaludů: Na Zbořenci 5, 120 00 Prague 2; U Jelínků: Charvátova 1, 110 00 Prague 1; U Rotundy: Karoliny Světlé 17, 110 00 Prague 1 | **Getting there** U Žaludů: tram 5, 17 to Jiráskovo náměstí, then walk along Záhořanského and Na Zderaze; U Jelínků: Metro B or tram 2, 9, 18, 22 to Národní třída, along Purkyňova and Vladislavova to Charvátova; U Rotundy: tram 2, 9, 18, 22 to Národní Divadlo, then to Smetanovo nábřeží, taking the narrow steps on the left to Divadelní, then Krocínova and Karoliny Světlé. | **Hours** U Žaludů: Mon–Fri 10.30am–11pm, Sat & Sun 11am–11pm; U Jelínků: Mon–Fri 10am–10pm, Sat & Sun 10am–6pm; U Rotundy: Mon–Fri 10am–10pm, Sat & Sun 11am–11pm | **Tip** To drink beer after 11pm, go to Restaurace U Kotvy at the corner of Spálená and Lazarská. As it's close to the all-night tram stop and is open late, this pub is the last port of call for Prague's night owls.

95 The Tomb of Westonia
The forgotten tenth muse

Almost all Czechs have heard of Edward Kelley, a famous alchemist who was active at the court of Rudolf II. During his lifetime, Kelley's stepdaughter was actually more famous than he was. Elizabeth Jane Weston, also known as Westonia, is regarded as the first woman poet from the region that is now the Czech Republic. She was known across Europe in the intellectual circles of her day.

Although Westonia was born in England and wrote in Latin, she spent most of her short, 31-year life in Bohemia. Shortly after her birth in 1581, her mother married Edward Talbot, alias Kelley, and together they travelled to central Europe to seek their fortune. Kelley established himself at the court of Emperor Rudolf II and acquired large estates, but his popularity gradually declined, and he ended up in prison after fighting a duel with a court official. His wealth was at an end, but young Westonia took advantage of her excellent education – which she owed to Kelley – and her talent as a writer, to send letters exhorting influential merchants to help her and to save the family from ruin. In 1602 her first collection of poems, *Poëmata*, was published, followed a short time later by *Parthenicôn*.

Westonia died in childbirth on 23 November, 1612 in Prague, and was buried in the Augustinian convent next to St Thomas' Church on Malá Strana. To see her gravestone, go through a door to the left of the nave of the church. It leads directly into the cloister. At the back of this is a slightly weathered stone plaque, on the upper part of which the name "Westonia" is still legible.

Contemporaries called her "the female Ovid" or "tenth muse," but today only experts on Latin humanist literature know of her. Equally forgotten is St Thomas's Church, which is adorned with faithful copies of two paintings by Peter Paul Rubens and works by Karel Škrétas.

Address Josefská 8, 118 00 Prague 1, www.augustiniani.cz | **Getting there** Tram 12, 15, 20, 22 to Malostranské náměstí, then go along Letenská and left into the one-way street Josefská | **Hours** Mass: Sun 9.30am & 6pm (in Czech), 11am (in English) & 12.30pm (in Spanish) | **Tip** Treat yourself to a cup of good coffee or home-made lemonade at Café Soda, Míšeňská 3. The colourful mixture of furniture, flowers and bikes leaning against the wall create a cosy living-room atmosphere.

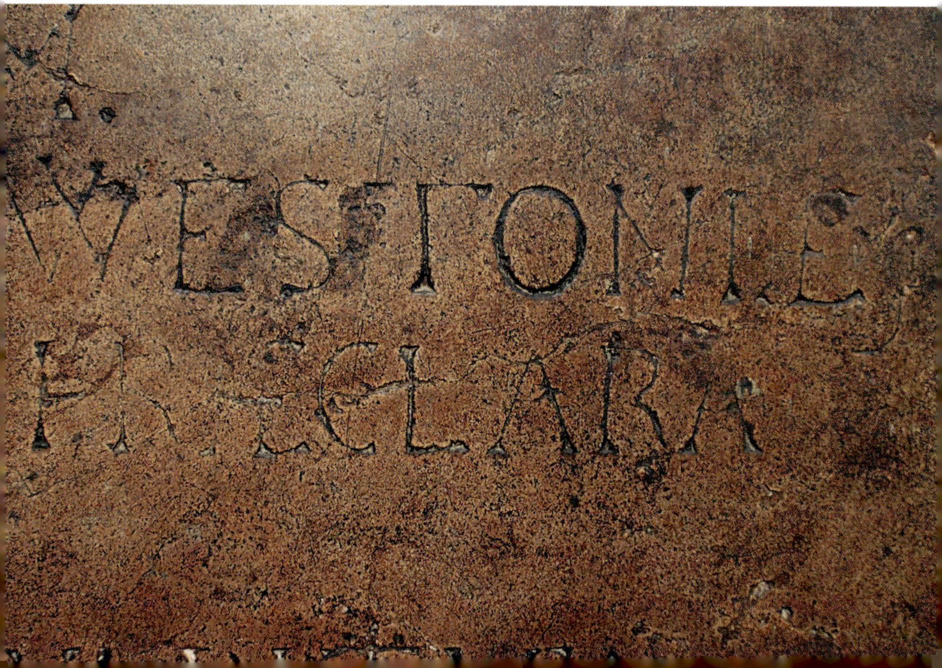

96__Toulcův dvůr

An organic farm amid the concrete

At Toulcův dvůr you might perhaps wish you were short-sighted, because if all the blocks of prefabricated concrete around you were blurred, you could remain under the illusion of being on a farmyard out in the country. But with communist urbanism breathing down your neck, Toulcův dvůr is a natural oasis in the city.

This "Centre for Ecological Education" occupies a ten-hectare site. The carefully restored historic farmyard and its adjacent agricultural buildings border an extensive area of green nature, with woodland, fields and meadows, orchards and grazing grounds. There is even some floodplain woodland here, which is periodically under water in spring, but dry enough again in summer for walking. Truly a complete natural habitat!

As the interesting information panels are only in Czech, it's a good idea to join the English-language guided tour. Then you'll learn about the "Noah's Ark Project." which has the aim of saving ancient breeds of Bohemian domestic animals from extinction: for example the Wallachian sheep, the huzule pony and Bohemian red cattle. It is not only people that wander around here: you will have the company of geese, hens and rabbits, which of course makes Toulcův dvůr attractive for children. Preschool and primary school classes from across Prague come here, and a kindergarten has been opened at the farmyard. Children can dig in the fields and learn what a cow really looks like.

However, this doesn't mean there's nothing for grown-ups. Regular country fairs, carnival parades, organic food markets and other seasonal events are held. There is a shop and a restaurant for organic food, and a mini-library. If you enjoy being woken in the morning by a crowing cockerel, book an overnight stay in one of the most characterful hostels in Prague, where a single room can be had for the sensationally low price of 350Kč per night.

Address Kubatova 32/1, 102 00 Prague 10, www.toulcuvdvur.cz | Getting there Metro A to Skalka, or metro C to Opatov, then from either of these bus 177 to Toulcův dvůr | Hours Farmyard and nature reserve: daily 8am–6pm | Tip It's also worth seeing what was left of Stará Hostivař after the demolition of the 1970s. There are enchanting spots around the village green and church, in the streets Selská, Domkářská, Mezi Potoky, Chalupnická, Kubatova and Přibíkova, and on the path by the Botič stream (between Kozinovo náměstí and K Horkám).

97__The Trojan Horse in Troy
It's not a joke!

In 2007, when the artist Ivan Nacvalač set up a huge wooden horse in the district called Troja (Troy), he was not primarily referring to the name of the area, which derives from the pseudo-antique decoration of its manor house. He simply wanted to create a pleasant spot. He constructed the nine-metre-tall horse, which is larger than the bronze horse on the Vítkov hill, in only three months, with the help of family and friends. The creature's belly was home to a gallery, which later spilled out on to the patch of land around the horse. Before very long a stage for concerts had been added, and between the horse's legs a little bar appeared, with a beer pump, a coffee machine and different kinds of rum from all over the world.

Later Nacvalač set up a mobile home next to the horse and moved into it. Unfortunately, during the floods of 2013 the home lived up to its name in terms of mobility and floated away – no one knows where it went. The horse survived the catastrophe unscathed, and so its creator simply went to live inside it instead. The art was taken outside, and today the open-air gallery occupies almost the whole garden. So not a lot has changed, apart from the path that now goes around the wooden horse. This is Prague's best-known cycle path, and amateur racers took a liking to it. But their inconsiderate behaviour, in and out of the saddle, soon got on Nacvalač's nerves. He decided to dry up their liquid supplies, and closed down his bar.

However, that doesn't mean that this agreeable man will send you away if you want to have a chat with him. On the contrary – jazz and blues concerts are still held around the horse, in an incomparable atmosphere. It's not only American expats who feel at home here. The musicians, too, enjoy themselves, and sometimes start a spontaneous jam session. By the way: does the name Laco Déczi mean anything to you?

Address Vodácká 1, 171 00 Prague 7 | **Getting there** Metro C to Nádraží Holešovice, then bus 112 to Kovárna, from Pod Havránkou turn left into Vodácká; or walk from Stromovka on Trojská lávka across the Emperor's Island (Císařský ostrov) | **Hours** See www.facebook.com/GalerieTrojskyKun | **Tip** A short distance from the Kovárna bus stop is an entrance to the Botanical Garden. Walk up through the vineyards to reach one of the city's loveliest parks, where you can sit on the broad lawns. Picnic blankets are available free of charge from the bistro.

98_ The Tunnel

A dare between Žižkov and Karlín

Drink a glass of schnapps in the Tachovské náměstí pub. Then take a deep breath, and set off through the 300-metre subterranean link between the districts of Žižkov and Karlín.

The tunnel has become much safer in recent years, so there's nothing to fear, at least during daylight hours. All the same, the ill-lit walk with its dull, yellow-grey ceramic tiles and faint ceiling lights will make you feel uneasy. After a few paces the noise of the city fades, and only the unsettling sounds from people walking ahead of or behind you disturb the silence. There isn't even light at the end of the tunnel, as it has a slightly crooked course. It's a popular location for films with junkie scenes.

Yet this tunnel for pedestrians and cyclists was built on a generous scale: it's between 4.4 and 4.8 metres wide, and up to 3.4 metres high. It was constructed in 1953 to shorten the journey to the factories in Karlín for workers from the densely populated Žižkov district. If you take the overground route across the Vítkov hill or the tram, this journey can easily last half an hour. Through the tunnel, however, it only takes a few minutes. It was only on the way home that the workers broke sweat, as there's an 8 percent gradient. So take care: cyclists whizz past at great speed.

As you exit at Karlín, note the doors. These lead to a labyrinth of passages and rooms, a Cold War nuclear bunker. They have their own supplies of water and power, so that 1,250 people could survive there for up to 72 hours, The city government still maintains this as a place of refuge in case of catastrophe, therefore it's not open to visitors. A moment later you're blinded by the daylight – and the tunnel is behind you.

Now it's time for a second schnapps. This is recommended by a tradition associated with the tunnel: first a drink for courage, then another when you emerge safely.

Address Entrance on the Žižkov side: Tachovské náměstí, 130 00 Prague 3; entrance on the Karlín side: Thámova, 186 00 Prague 8 | **Getting there** Metro C to Florenc, then bus 133 or 207 to Tachovské náměstí; or metro B to Křižíkova, then walk along Thámova | **Tip** The Žižkov entrance is close to the Vítkov hill, site of a gigantic Modernist monument that was once also the mausoleum of the first communist president, Klement Gottwald. Exhibitions are held today in the huge, dark, musty rooms. There is also a colossal equestrian statue of Jan Žižka (leader of the Hussite army), a café and a superb view of Prague.

99 __ U Apolináře

A Gothic-style maternity clinic

On a dull November day the sight of its gloomy silhouette could send a shiver down your spine: this is dark romanticism in its purest form. Nevertheless, for 140 years many citizens of Prague have had their most joyful moments here. The U Apolináře maternity clinic was one of the first of its kind, and although it has state-of-the-art equipment today, you could easily imagine *Oliver Twist* being set here: there are similar stories in its history.

The clinic's predecessor, a maternity hospital with an orphanage for the poor, was built in 1789, not far from the Church of St Apollinaris. In the 19th century the decision was taken to rebuild it, and the commission was awarded to Josef Hlávka, who had also built the Vienna State Opera. His task was not to design an attractive building, but a hospital where infection wouldn't spread. It was not then known that the main cause of puerperal fever was the unwashed hands of midwives and their assistants. As his building material Hlávka therefore used naked, unplastered brick, which was considered to be the safest option. As a further precautionary measure, the hospital was designed as a system of six pavilions that could each be isolated in case of an epidemic.

The maternity clinic, which opened in 1875, was then Europe's largest such facility. It took in both poor and rich women. If the latter had an unwanted pregnancy, they could enter the building through a side entrance; there were two wards where they could give birth in secret.

Don't miss the entrance hall of the clinic, where you're welcomed by a mannequin of a pregnant woman in a polka-dot nightdress, and a bright vaulted ceiling with brick arches. The glass door leads to an enclosed courtyard. After the intimidating façade, it offers a pleasant breath of air. And if you want to visit the hospital, you don't have to be an expectant mother.

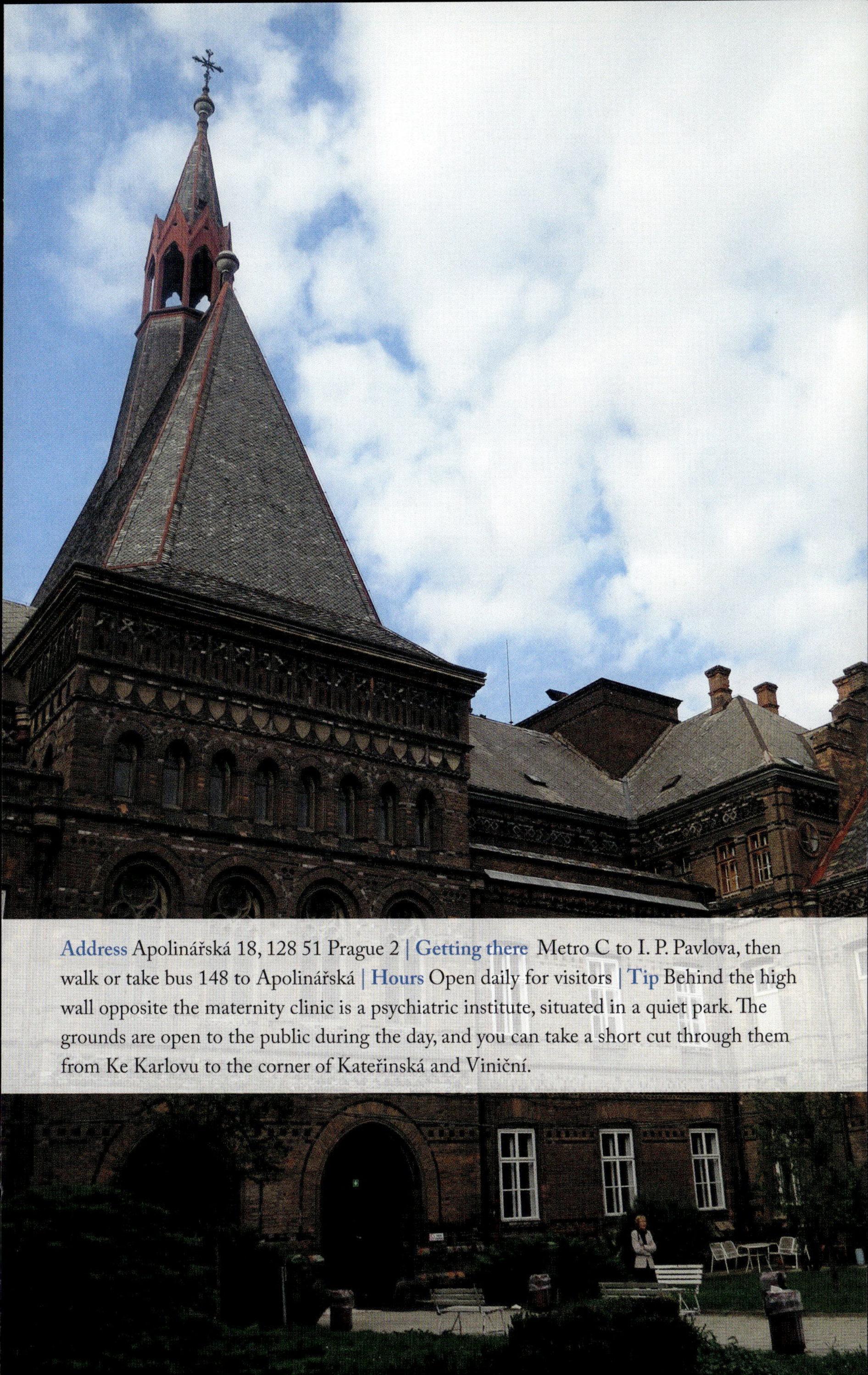

Address Apolinářská 18, 128 51 Prague 2 | Getting there Metro C to I. P. Pavlova, then walk or take bus 148 to Apolinářská | Hours Open daily for visitors | Tip Behind the high wall opposite the maternity clinic is a psychiatric institute, situated in a quiet park. The grounds are open to the public during the day, and you can take a short cut through them from Ke Karlovu to the corner of Kateřinská and Viniční.

100___U Budyho
The legacy of the long-haired

They say U Budyho is in a world of its own – but that's an over-simplification. This is a pub where several worlds meet in a remarkable way.

It belongs to Petr Placák, a publicist who was a key figure in the illegal opposition of the late 1980s. At that time he played in the famous underground band the Plastic People of the Universe. He wrote lyrics, organised demonstrations, and in 1988 founded an initiative that was openly critical of the regime. Today he edits the magazine *Babylon*, which focusses on the influence of communism on present-day Czech society. Since 2010 the unofficial headquarters of the magazine has been the U Budyho pub.

On three sides it is surrounded by allotments. This is truly ironic: during the years of "normalisation" after the Prague Spring, nothing was as symbolic of people's retreat into private life, or so diametrically opposed to the political underground, as the state-subsidised cultivation of gardens. Today, however, the amateur gardeners and former long-haired dissidents live together in harmony; well-tended plots assert their petit bourgeois presence alongside the extensive plot of land around the pub, where mowing the lawn is the last thing that would occur to anyone. It's a venue for concerts and readings, or for playing foot tennis. Trippers sometimes take a break here.

Perhaps one day even the residents of the luxury flats that are going up nearby will yield to the charm of the relaxed atmosphere: beer-garden benches beneath a corrugated-iron roof, tables and chairs that came from heaven knows where, toilets with "character," and the original wooden house dating from 1940 – where in winter visitors can have a really good time, feeling like scouts inside their hut. Everything is run by a landlord nicknamed Red Ruda, an ex-miner who was homeless before Placák employed and accommodated him here.

Address Menclova, 180 00 Prague 8 | **Getting there** Tram 1, 6, 14, 25 to Libeňský most; opposite the tram stop, steps lead down to Libeňský ostrov; go straight ahead here to Residenz Dock. Opposite, a little path leads from Menclova to U Budyho. | **Hours** Mon–Fri 2–10pm, Sat & Sun 11am–10pm, but closing time depends on the number of customers | **Tip** Go back a little way to Libeňský most to see the Olgoj Chorchoj architecture and design studio. Note the statues around it, mostly connected with sport. They are the work of the Czech sculptor Zdeněk Němeček.

The U Elektry Flea Market

Marketplace for the wild east

Again and again during the communist period, the Prague police persisted in breaking up the illegal trade in vinyl records by bands from the West, as well as other rare and forbidden goods from the other side of the Iron Curtain. The regime was utterly convinced that it could suppress the entrepreneurial spirit.

Yet it's precisely those markets that were once hounded by the state which are now regarded as the ancestors of U Elektry, the biggest flea market in the Czech Republic and, according to its website, perhaps the biggest in Europe. But if you expect to stroll and browse in romantic surroundings, where you can buy antiques and curiosities in a pleasant neighbourhood atmosphere, this is not the place for you. Every Saturday and Sunday, over an area of 50,000 square metres, you can find anything and everything that you need: garden equipment, clothes, electronics, car tyres, tools, toiletries and even food. Among the brand-new products there are of course lots of the second-hand items and antiques that make up a classic flea market. Some sellers present their wares on stands or in huts that they rent on a long-term basis, while others display their goods in a car boot or lay them out on a carpet on the ground. Most of the dealers are Czech, but you'll also come across a few Poles, sometimes Germans and Austrians, and – if you're really lucky – a Russian priest who'll sell you some jam. Some sellers are very willing to bargain over the price, while others simply refuse to haggle. The flea market in U Elektry is no smooth and shiny operation where everything goes to plan, but a living organism that changes and evolves.

The market was founded in 2003 by two traders, partly because they were unwilling to accept the disappearance of the old marketplaces, but also because they couldn't face the thought of suddenly having a free weekend.

Address U Elektry 888/3, 190 00 Prague 9, www.blesitrhy.cz | **Getting there** Metro B to Palmovka, tram 8, 25 to Nademlejnská, then go back a little way on the main road and turn left | **Hours** Sat & Sun 7am–1.30pm | **Tip** If you continue along U Elektry, pass beneath the railway tracks and go left into Mezitraťová, you enter a completely different world: close to the allotment gardens, on the site of a bloody battle in the Seven Years' War (1756–63), the Rokytka stream flows in impressive, though man-made meanders.

 The U Prince Terrace

The mother of all views

Old Town Square – this means masses of tourists, and the crowds become even denser as the time approaches for the astronomical clock on the town hall to strike the hour. But if you hate being caught in a crush and would like to see the square from a different perspective, there is an attractive option: though you can't see it from below, the U Prince Hotel opposite the town hall has a terrace, that users of the Trivago website have voted one of the 15 best hotel roof terraces in the world.

On the way up to the fourth floor, the glass lift at the end of the entrance lobby shows you the splendid interior of this 12th-century building that is now a five-star hotel. The façade of the burgher's house originally known as The Golden Angel (or The Black Angel) was remodelled in the Baroque style in the 18th century, but inside there are still Gothic stone doorways, and there's a well in what is now the cellar bar.

When you leave the lift, you have to climb a few steps in order to reach the open-air restaurant. It's not among the best in Prague, nor is it one of the cheapest, but to make up for this you have a fantastic view of the town hall and the Týn Church on one side, and of the castle and the Petřín observation tower on the other. The panorama alone, of the roofs, towers and churches of the Old Town, is breathtaking, which is why the terrace is so popular with both Czech and international film-makers.

The restaurant is open all year round. It seats 90 in winter, and when the weather is bad most of it is covered, and guests are kept warm with blankets and radiator lamps. However, the best time for taking a seat up here is in summer, when you can enjoy the view over an ice-cold cocktail. This is not too hard on the wallet, and if you have a camera with you, you will leave the terrace with picture-postcard shots of the city of Prague.

Address Staroměstské náměstí 29, 110 00 Prague 1, www.terasauprince.com | **Getting there** Metro A, B to Můstek, then through Na Můstku and Melantrichova to Staroměstské náměstí | **Hours** Daily 11am – 11.30pm; after 3pm it's advisable to book a table | **Tip** Close to Old Town Square and well hidden from the tourists lies Týnská literární kavárna (Týnská 6). This literary café is popular with students, artists and writers. In summer its courtyard is possibly the pleasantest place to sit in the city centre.

103 The Velodrome
Nostalgia in Třebešín

Perhaps you're not a dyed-in-the-wool fan of track cycling – because it's so boring when they just ride round in a circle. But give it a chance: the oldest cycle-racing track in the Czech Republic is sure to arouse your enthusiasm. The oval track may have seen better days, but it's still functioning, and it possesses a charm that's difficult to describe – perhaps because it was built not by an official association but by fans, for whom an outing on a bike without brakes meant one thing above all: boundless speed.

The velodrome is the venue for the world's second-oldest sprint event, after the Grand Prix de Paris: the Framar bike race. This was established in 1938 by František Martínek, a paint wholesaler and five times winner of the Czech championship. At that time it was still a road race in the Pankrác district. Three years later it moved to the racetrack in Třebešín, then 412 metres long with moderate bends. It was built in only four months by the engineer Josef Šídlo, a bike racer himself, and his friends from the sport. The enthusiasm of these sports fanatics was greater than their technical skill: after only a few years, the track was falling apart. It was rebuilt, with its current length of 333 metres and an angle of 34 degrees in the bends. Apart from the Framar race, the Czech championships are also held here.

Despite this, the whole complex has a neglected look. The building that used to be a hotel and also housed changing rooms for the riders is dilapidated, and has been awaiting restoration for years. The subway leading under the cycle track to the grass in the middle, once used for greyhound races, is flooded, and the whole site is overgrown with bushes. But it's precisely this that gives the track its shabby-chic character, and serves as a reminder of the days when the sport was dominated not by professional clubs, but enthusiastic fans.

214

Address Nad Kapličkou 15, 100 00 Prague 10 | **Getting there** Metro B, C to Florenc, then bus 133 to Třebešín, and go along K Červenému dvoru and Na Třebešíně | **Hours** Members of the Kovo youth sport centre train in the velodrome. It is open to the public for races: for dates, see www.kovopraha.cz. | **Tip** Near the velodrome are interesting villas that used to belong to well-known people. The house at Slunečná 21 was built in the 1960s by the architect Jiří Siegl for the singer Karel Gott. The villa in late Modernist style at Na Třebešíně 16 was once home to the writer František Kožík, and the actor Jaroslav Marvan lived at K Červenému dvoru 1.

104___Větrník

Prague's only remaining windmill

When people from Prague hear the word "Větrník," the first thing that occurs to them is a famous dessert, and secondly they might think of a student quarter between Břevnov and Petřiny. Not many people know that "Větrník" also used to mean "windmill" – nor that one of these is still standing in Břevnov.

This lovely building, beautifully restored to its original condition, has kept its cylindrical shape. However its characteristic sails are now missing, because by the late 19th century it was no longer being used for its original purpose. The mill was probably built in 1722 by Kilian Ignaz Dientzenhofer, which makes it one of the oldest remaining mills in Bohemian lands. But its history goes back much further: according to various engravings, a wooden mill belonging to the Břevnov Monastery once stood on the site. The old mill was used for much more than grinding flour. It also operated as a sawmill, and raised water from a well for the monastery orchard.

The well is still in use today; it yields enough water to supply the guesthouse that occupies the mill and the adjacent buildings. The guesthouse is run by the Opatrný family, descendants of a restaurant owner named Josef Černohorský, who bought Větrník in 1899 and converted it into a restaurant for day trippers. However, its period of prosperity ended in 1929, with the owner's death. After that, the family occupied the premises as a fine residence. This period came to a close when the communists took power, and against the owner's wishes, tenants were brought in. They carried out a number of poor quality alterations. To enable them to reverse these and to restore the whole site, the Opatrnýs run a guesthouse on part of the premises. In 2013 they also revived their ancestor's trade by opening a restaurant, which is growing ever more popular. By the way: you can eat the other kind of Větrník here.

Address U Větrníku 40/1, 162 00 Prague 6, www.restauracevetrnik.cz | **Getting there** Metro A to Hradčanská, then tram 1 or 2 to Větrník, and go along Ankarská and Za Zahradou | **Hours** Daily 11am–10pm | **Tip** Just one tram stop further out of the city, to the right of the main road, is an estate designed by the architect Vlado Milunić, who also jointly designed the famous Dancing House. Walking there, you can't help thinking how much nicer Prague would be if all its housing estates looked like this.

105 The Vietnamese Sapa Market

The aroma of green coriander

While London, New York and Vancouver all have their famous Chinatown districts, Prague can boast of its Little Hanoi – at Sapa, in the district of Libuš on the edge of the city. For size and atmosphere it beats all the other Vietnamese markets in the Czech Republic. So save yourself the cost of a 15-hour long-distance flight: if you want to inhale the aromas of South-East Asia, it's quite enough to travel half an hour out of the city centre.

The beginnings of the market go back to 1999, when a Vietnamese company bought a site that had belonged to a meat collective and poultry farm. Market stalls loaded with hundreds of T-shirts, jeans and handbags sprang up on the more than 35-hectare site. A supermarket, school, Buddhist temple, offices and Vietnamese magazine publishers are also based on the premises, where around 7,000 Vietnamese live and work today. When you pass through the red gate, the first impression you get is of one huge car park. Vans and trucks weave their way between halls with corrugated-iron roofs, as people from all over the country come to make purchases here. Forget about traffic signs – you have to assert yourself. Lots of bicycles are on the move, too, pedalled by traders taking lunch back to their stalls.

But we almost forgot: food! You can spice up your diet here with lemongrass, Thai basil and many kinds of rice noodles, and also sample authentic Asian meals. The small family bistros offer only one or two dishes, but these are cooked to perfection. The grilled pork belly in sweet-and-sour sauce at Hai Ha is famous. So are the spring rolls at Phuong Phuong and the grilled duck at Dung Lien. If you prefer your tables to be wiped down from time to time, then don't look too closely. Just close your eyes and breathe in the aroma of strong meat broth and coriander. This can't be anywhere but Hanoi, can it?

Address TTTM Sapa, Libušská 319/126, 142 00 Prague 4, www.informace-sapa.cz & www.sapa-praha.cz | **Getting there** Metro C to Kačerov, then bus 113 or metro B to Smíchovské nádraží, then bus 197, in both cases to Sídliště Písnice | **Hours** 8am–6pm, restaurants and casinos until 10pm | **Tip** As the range of stalls and restaurants at Sapa is truly enormous, have a look at www.sapamapa.cz to get your bearings. Then you can head straight for your favourite stall.

106_ Villa Štvanice

Actors from the sad island

If you ask the actors sitting at the bar what was in this building before, they'll shrug their shoulders and say, "Flood water." A succinct reply, but in fact it says everything. The history of this interesting classical house is largely unknown; its crumbling plaster and bare ceilings are the result of the two major floods that have already afflicted Prague in this millennium.

The first and more serious inundation in 2002 drove the last tenants out of the building, and no one has lived in it since then. In 2013 a list of endangered historic monuments on the internet attracted the attention of a group of actors, who then put on an interactive performance about the Golem in the house. They liked the villa so much that they rented it from the city authorities for five years. At present three theatre ensembles are established here. Each of them has a different specialisation, but all three have a liking for things outside the ordinary. There's a large room with a capacity for an audience of 60, as well as rehearsal space and a pleasant café run by the actors.

They've succeeded in creating a cultural oasis in the middle of the city. Apart from the tennis court, there's not much else of interest round here, except perhaps the skate park, which is said to be one of the best in Europe. Then there are some poorly tended gardens and the decaying bike park, the remains of the famous winter stadium that was demolished in 2011. Prague's second-biggest island is enveloped in an air of gloom and sadness.

It wasn't always like this,though. In bygone days, the people of Prague came here for relaxation and entertainment. After 1989 there were plans to revitalise the island, but nothing came of them. And so the history of Villa Štvanice remains an object lesson in showing that real enthusiasm can achieve so much more than even the best plans of the authorities.

Address Ostrov Štvanice 858, 170 00 Prague 7, www.vilastvanice.cz | **Getting there** Metro B, C to Florenc, then go along Ke Štvanici, on to the bridge Hlávkův most, down the steps to the island and along the path beneath the bridge | **Hours** Café: Wed – Sun from 2pm, or one hour before the start of performances | **Tip** At the tip of Štvanice island is an Art Nouveau electricity plant dating from 1913. From this side you have a view of the imposing glass door and part of the turbine, which rises above the water on a base. The tower and dome, inspired by French chateau architecture, can be seen from the nearby Nábřeží Ludvíka Svobody embankment.

107 The Vltava Sauna

Cool off with the swans

Are you a sauna fan? Then you really must sweat a while on the Vltava river! For the last few years, there's been a wooden sauna cabin in winter on the deck of the *(A)void*, a ship moored at Výtoň.

You sit at temperatures of 90 degrees Celsius only a few metres above the water level and, as the sweat pours off your back, through the glass wall of the boat you can see trippers on the river, trains thundering across the nearby railway bridge and the majestic panorama of Prague's castle. But best of all, there are swans! Sometimes they come in a great flock and cover the surface of the water, white dots as far as the eye can see. You can even join them to cool off – the ladder that leads straight down into the icy waters is one of the highlights of the sauna. For those who don't fancy the chilly Vltava, a bucket of cold tap water is at the ready. And don't worry: a screen conceals you from the prying eyes of passers-by on the Rašín embankment.

Similar facilities can be found on the rivers of other cities, but what distinguishes the ship sauna in Prague from others is its small size (it has a maximum capacity of 15 sauna guests), an atmosphere of enthusiasm and a certain underground feeling. No wonder: the sauna was first set up here in 2009 by two young architects from the studio H3T, who harboured a longing to get warm all the way through during Prague's winters. They initially lived out their passion in a series of projects such as the mobile sauna that used to stand on the square in front of the New Scene at the National Theatre, and a cabin that could be pulled behind a bicycle as a trailer. The sauna on the ship made it clear to the architects that they were not the only ones who enjoyed sweating in strange places. It's just a pity that their sauna on the *(A)void* has to be dismantled every spring, to make way for more profitable activities.

Address Deck of the ship (A)void, Rašínovo nábřeží, 120 00 Prague 2 | **Getting there** Tram 2, 3, 7, 17, 21 to Výtoň; the ship is moored close to the tram stop | **Hours** Oct–Apr (depending on the weather) daily 6–11pm, booking recommended: www.laznenalodi.cz | **Tip** Before you leave, stop in the pleasant bar on board the (A)void. Concerts, readings and other cultural events sometimes take place here.

108__VýLetná
More than tennis

In 1904 the famous Lawn Tennis Club Praha on the Letná was founded by law students. It quickly gained favour with Prague's high society. People like Jan and Olga Masaryk, children of the first president of Czechoslovakia, Jiří Stanislav Guth-Jarkovský, chairman of the Czechoslovakian Olympic Committee, and Prince Karel VI Schwarzenberg, father of the politician, all met with racquet in hand at the LTC. Czech professionals also trained here, for example Tomáš Šmíd, a member of the victorious Davis Cup team in 1980.

It's all over now – game, set and match. Before the fall of communism the club was still in business, although it lacked proper legal status and operated under changing names, but after 1989 a conflict that continues to this day began to rage around the shabby wooden clubhouse, which was constructed in 1926 to designs by Bohumír Kozák. Although the building was a protected heritage site, its days seemed numbered. In 2014, however, hope of salvation appeared: while legal proceedings continued, the club premises were taken over by a society named Alternativa II. They are attempting to save it with the help of volunteers, their own financial resources, various fund-raising activities and the revenue from paintball played in the adjacent hall.

The building is worth saving. There's a smell of wood from its cladding of dark battens and its white window frames. To the left are four outdoor courts with stands, now in use again. Players have changing rooms and can leave their clothes in the original lockers, now renovated. After a game, the best place to eat is the clubhouse lounge. The rest awaits restoration.

If you play tennis, like historic buildings or simply enjoy a walk in the park, VýLetná is definitely worth a visit. Apart from its pleasant atmosphere, you will have the agreeable feeling of contributing to the revival of a famous place.

Address Letenské sady 32, 170 00 Prague 7, www.vyletna.info | **Getting there** Tram 1, 8, 12, 25, 26 to Letenské náměstí, then go along Ovenecká and Muzejní to the entrance to Letenské sady | **Hours** During the season, daily 11am – 11pm (longer if required) | **Tip** Some of the tennis courts fell victim to construction of the Letná Tunnel in the 1950s. Thanks to their geometric mosaics by the painter Zdeněk Sýkora, the ventilation towers of the tunnel are works of art. They're next to the park entrance, opposite the National Museum for Agriculture and National Technical Museum.

109_ The Water Tunnel
Back to the roots

Everyone knows the Charles Bridge. But not many realise that this landmark of the city conceals a water tunnel with a length of 120 metres on the Old Town side. On a boat you can pass under an unknown arch of the Charles Bridge, and also beneath the Romanesque vaults of the Judith Bridge, its 12th century predecessor.

If you stand on Křižovnické náměstí, it looks as if the end of the Charles Bridge is beyond the bridge tower. However, beneath the square flows a channel of the Vltava that once served as a mill stream for the Old Town mills on what is now Novotného lávka. When the statue of Charles IV was erected in the 19th century, an embankment was built and the last arch of the Judith Bridge filled in. The square was extended – and the water tunnel was created.

It's accessed through an iron gate next to the Church of St Francis of Assisi. The annoying thing is that there is a mooring of the Pražské Benátky boat company in the tunnel. As soon as you approach the gate, a promoter wearing a sailor's outfit will give you his sales spiel. This is probably why even Prague natives don't know the water tunnel: they scent a tourist trap, want to avoid pickpockets, and walk across the crowded square as fast as they can.

Yet a boat trip through the tunnel definitely has its charm. The damp stones of the Judith Bridge exude a whiff of the Middle Ages, and from a boat you get an unusual view of the Charles Bridge, as well as the best angle for seeing Malá Strana and the castle. You can either board a pedalo, which can be hired from the nearby Klub Lávka, or one of the boats of Pražské Benátky. Although the quality of their explanations is poor, your boat ticket also gives you admission to the Charles Bridge Museum. Here, in the basement, you can admire the lower part of the Church of St Francis of Assisi and the foundations of the Judith Bridge.

Address Křižovnické náměstí, 110 00 Prague 1, Klub Lávka: Novotného lávka 1, www.lavka.cz; Muzeum Karlova Mostu: www.muzeumkarlovamostu.cz | **Getting there** Metro A to Staroměstská; tram 2, 17, 18 to Karlovy lázně | **Hours** The Pražské Benátky boats run from 10.30am to 6pm every 15–20 minutes, depending on the season (www.prazskebenatky.cz) | **Tip** The stone relief of a bearded man called Bradáč was a flood warning in the Middle Ages. If the water reached his beard, it was time to evacuate the Old Town. Bradáč is on the quay wall of Křižovnické náměstí, having been moved there in the 19th century from a pier of the Judith Bridge. A copy is in its original position, on the right next to the steps that lead to the Pražské Benátky mooring.

110 The Waterworks in Vršovice

Water, technology, elegance

Strangely, the Vršovice waterworks consists of two plants – one of them is in Michle, the other in Braník. In the early 20th century, the town of Vršovice needed to ensure an adequate water supply, but there was no high ground within the municipal boundary from where water could flow by gravity feed through pipes down to the Vršovice plain. An agreement was therefore made with the town of Michle to build a water tower there. The pumping station was constructed in Braník, a neighbouring district. Everyone benefited, as the waterworks supplied three districts and also Krč, through which the pipeline was put.

The waterworks is a fine building, designed by Jan Kotěra, who is often described as the founder of modern Czech architecture. He chose an elegant geometric Art Nouveau style for the structure of plain brick with green-glazed decoration.

The 42-metre-high tapering tower that holds the water tanks stands in Michle. The coat of arms of Vršovice adorns the entrance with its granite steps. The tower remained in use until 1975, and its subterranean reservoir still functions. This is why the plant is not open to the public. The tower can only be viewed from the gate in Hanusova street or from the entrance in Pod Vršovickou vodárnou III. It's a sublime sight, though rather a sad one, as the tower is decaying more and more. In spring 2016 scaffolding appeared…

If you would like an impression of what Kotěra's brick façades looked like when they were first built, pay a visit to the former pumping station in Braník. This was the first place where water was chlorinated in Czechoslovakia. This plant too was decommissioned in the 1970s. In 2011 it was restored and converted into a leisure facility for children. In the restaurant, don't forget to look up: the original track for the crane can still be seen in what used to be the engine room.

Address Water tower: Hanusova 5, 140 00 Prague 4; Pumping station: Vltavanů 229, 147 00 Prague 4 | **Getting there** Water tower: metro C to Pankrác, then walk or take bus 134 to Zelená liška; Pumping station: tram 2, 3, 17, 21 to Nádraží Braník | **Hours** Pumping station: daily 9am–8pm | **Tip** Near the waterworks in Braník is an architecturally interesting brewery (Údolní 212). The company logo by Mikoláš Aleš showing St Wenceslas and two angels is still visible on the main building.

111   Ztracenka Park

Forgotten beneath the castle wall

It is almost incomprehensible that Ztracenka – the "Lost Park" – is known only to a few local residents and students at the nearby Albertov campus. The reason may be that the park hasn't been in existence for very long. The steep, narrow plot of land between the city wall of Prague's New Town and the walls of the former Augustinian monastery was once an orchard and a vineyard.

Before 1989 primary school children played here in their breaks, and then the garden was allowed to grow wild – a forgotten, hidden paradise. Its reconstruction, which was completed in 2010, created a dense network of small paths and brick terraces that crisscross the park. They were inspired by the Baroque terraces beneath the castle, and now visitors can relax there and enjoy a wonderful view over the city, just as they can from the castle.

If Ztracenka itself is a tip for insiders, then the nearby skittle alley and snack bar are almost completely unknown – although they're only a few paces away. All you have to do is walk a few metres further along Horská ulice and turn right through a little gate. Standing in front of the low wooden hut, you might feel as though you're in one of the melancholy paintings of Kamil Lhoták. Although this place is actually a private club, anyone at all can order a glass of beer or something to eat on the terrace. According to the management, the opening times depend on the weather.

When you've had your refreshments, it's time for a game of skittles, which has been played here since the 1930s. Players maintain that it's primarily a sport, and not just a way of having fun, like bowling. At first glance, it differs from bowling chiefly in that the balls don't have holes in them.

As there are repeated (though so far unspecific) rumours that this historic skittle alley is to be demolished, you really ought to try your hand while you still can!

Address Horská entrance, 128 00 Prague 2 | **Getting there** Tram 7, 14, 18, 24 to Albertov, then go along Horská ulice. The second entrance to the park is behind the Mathematical-Physical Faculty of the Charles University Ke Karlovu. | **Hours** Ztracenka Park: May–Sept 8am–8pm; Oct–Apr 8am–6pm; skittle alley (*kuželník*): Tue–Thu 3pm–midnight; on other days, book through Mr Smékal: Tel. +420/608877866 | **Tip** There's a special atmosphere in Albertov, the only district of Prague that could be described as a university campus. At the corner of Albertov and Studničkova, two plaques commemorate the student march that began the Velvet Revolution in 1989.

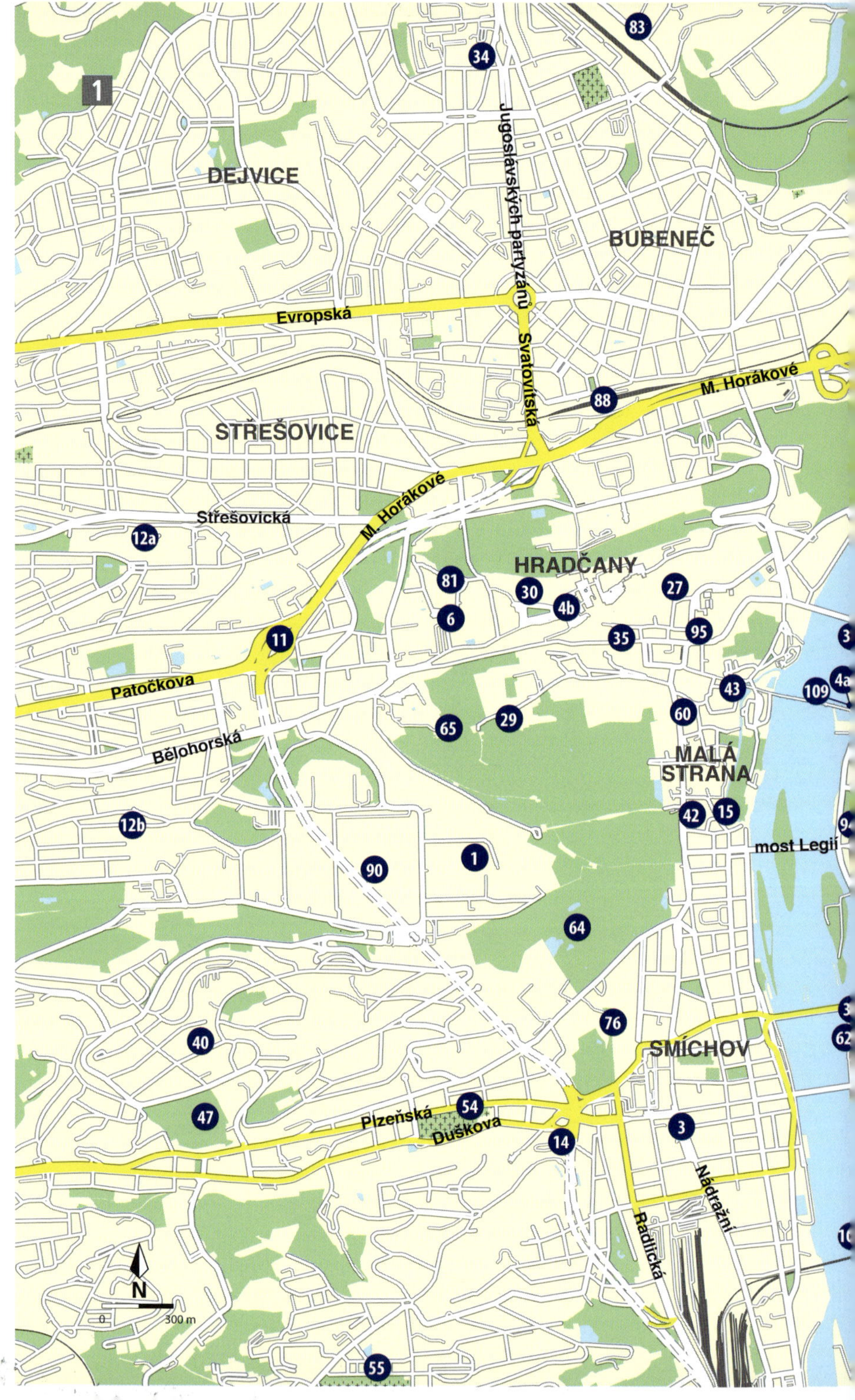

1
DEJVICE
BUBENEČ
STŘEŠOVICE
HRADČANY
MALÁ STRANA
SMÍCHOV
Evropská
Jugoslávských partyzánů
Svatovítská
M. Horákové
M. Horákové
M. Horákové
Střešovická
Patočkova
Bělohorská
most Legií
Plzeňská
Duškova
Radlická
Nádražní
N
0   300 m
34
83
88
12a
81
30
4b
27
6
35
95
11
43
109
4a
3
60
65
29
42
15
9
1
90
64
76
3
62
40
3
47
54
14
3
55
10

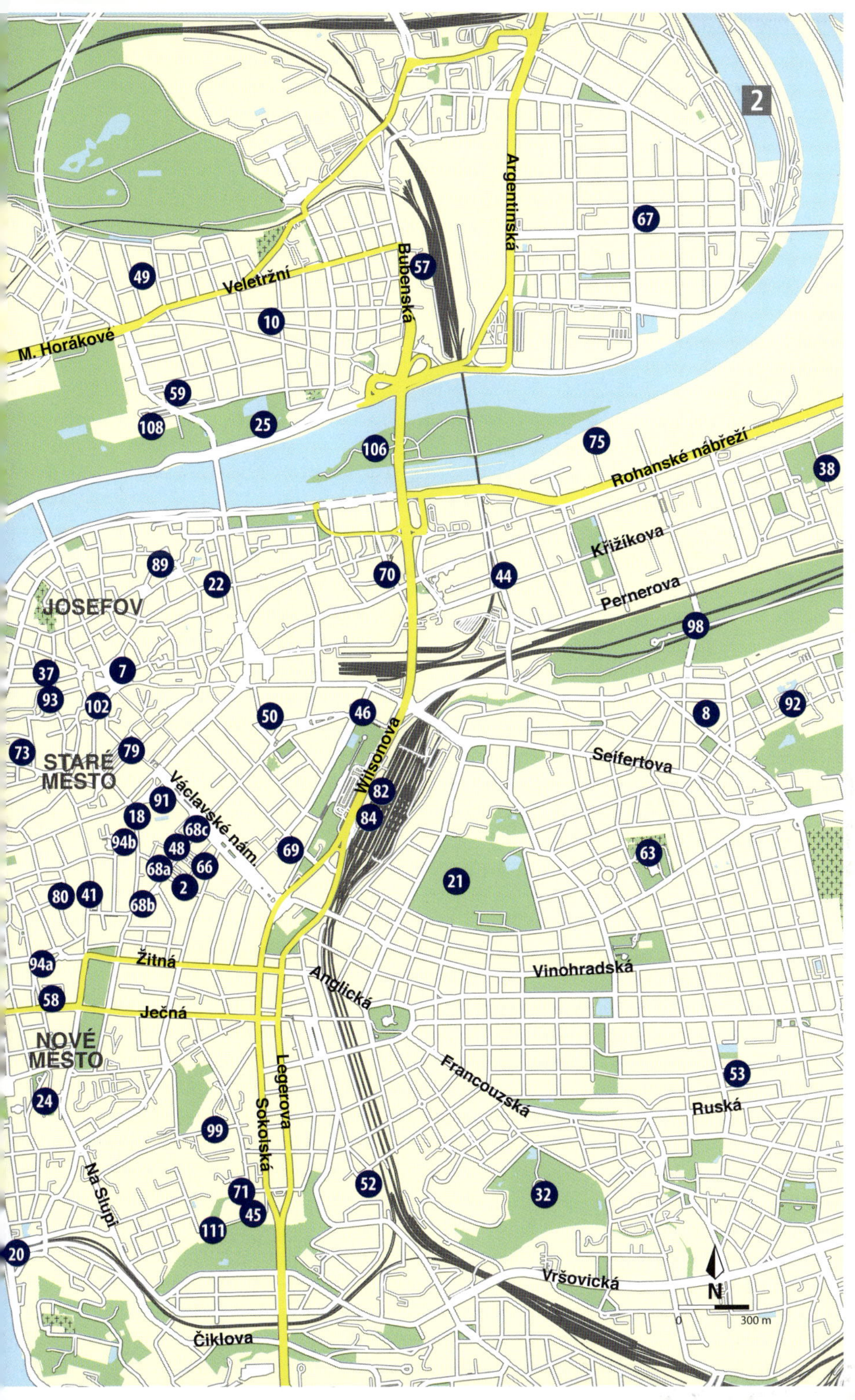

2
67
Argentinská
Bubenská
57
49
Veletržní
10
M. Horákové
59
108
25
106
75
Rohanské nábřeží
38
Křižíkova
89
22
70
44
Pernerova
JOSEFOV
98
37
7
93
102
8
92
73
50
46
STARÉ
79
Seifertova
MĚSTO
Wilsonova
91
Václavské nám.
18
82
63
94b
68c
84
48
69
68a
66
21
80
41
2
68b
94a
Žitná
Vinohradská
58
Anglická
Ječná
NOVÉ
MĚSTO
Legerova
Sokolská
Francouzská
53
24
Ruská
99
52
71
32
45
111
20
Vršovická
N
Na Slupi
Čiklova
300 m

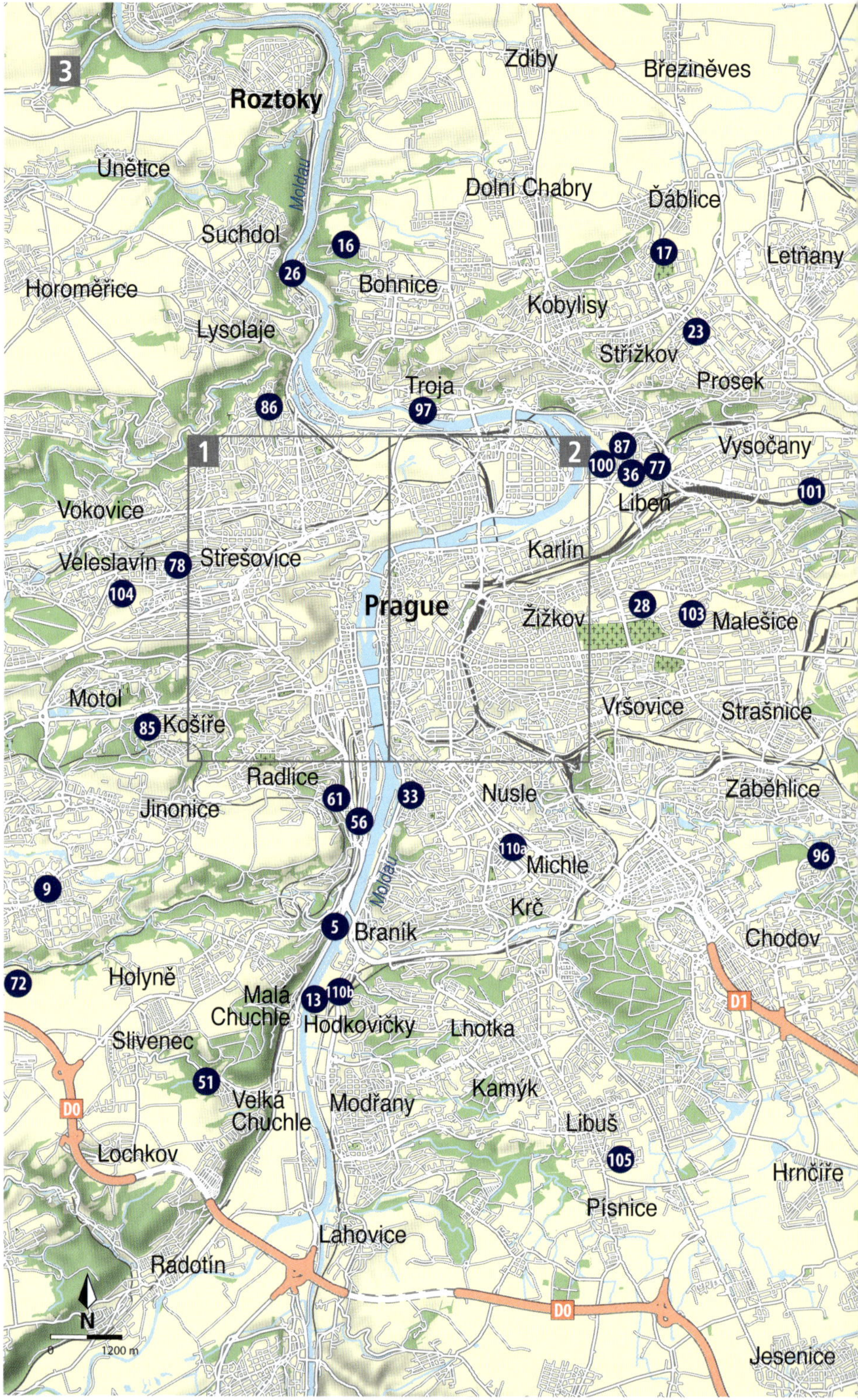

3
Roztoky
Únětice
Suchdol
Horoměřice
Lysolaje
Bohnice
Dolní Chabry
Ďáblice
Letňany
Kobylisy
Střížkov
Prosek
Troja
Vysočany
Liben
Karlín
Vokovice
Veleslavín
Střešovice
Prague
Žižkov
Malešice
Vršovice
Strašnice
Motol
Košíře
Radlice
Nusle
Záběhlice
Jinonice
Michle
Krč
Chodov
Braník
Holyně
Malá
Chuchle
Hodkovičky
Lhotka
Kamýk
Slivenec
Libuš
Hrnčíře
Velká
Chuchle
Modřany
Lochkov
Písnice
Lahovice
Radotín
Jesenice
Moldau
N
1200 m

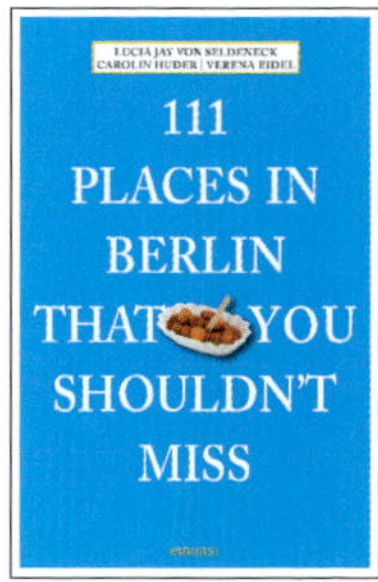

Lucia Jay von Seldeneck,
Carolin Huder, Verena Eidel
**111 PLACES IN BERLIN
THAT YOU SHOULDN'T MISS**
ISBN 978-3-95451-208-9

Rüdiger Liedtke
**111 PLACES IN MUNICH
THAT YOU SHOULDN'T MISS**
ISBN 978-3-95451-222-5

Rike Wolf
**111 PLACES IN HAMBURG
THAT YOU SHOULDN'T MISS**
ISBN 978-3-95451-234-8

Paul Kohl
**111 PLACES IN BERLIN
ON THE TRAIL OF THE NAZIS**
ISBN 978-3-95451-323-9

Sharon Fernandes
**111 PLACES IN NEW DELHI
THAT YOU MUST NOT MISS**
ISBN 978-3-95451-648-3

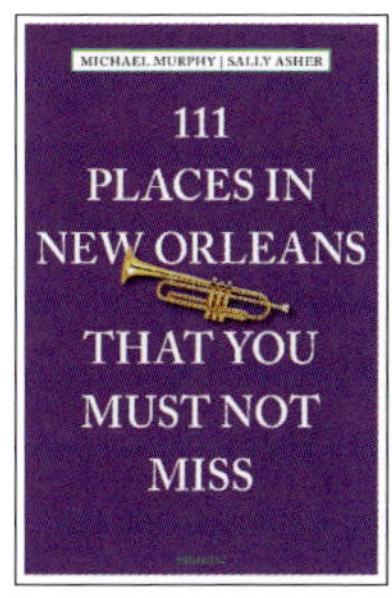

Sally Asher, Michael Murphy
**111 PLACES IN NEW ORLEANS
THAT YOU MUST NOT MISS**
ISBN 978-3-95451-645-2

Dirk Engelhardt
**111 PLACES IN BARCELONA
THAT YOU MUST NOT MISS**
ISBN 978-3-95451-353-6

Rüdiger Liedtke
**111 PLACES ON MALLORCA
THAT YOU SHOULDN'T MISS**
ISBN 978-3-95451-281-2

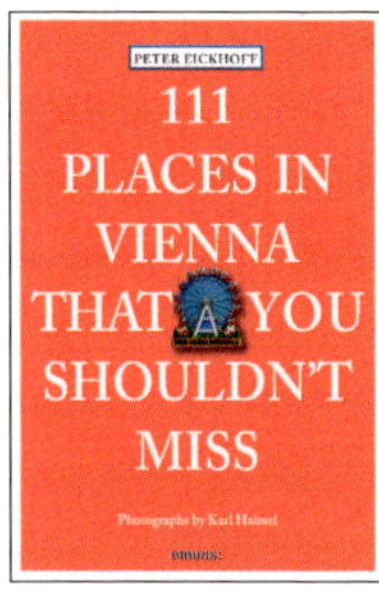

Peter Eickhoff
**111 PLACES IN VIENNA
THAT YOU SHOULDN'T MISS**
ISBN 978-3-95451-206-5

Frank McNally
**111 PLACES IN DUBLIN
THAT YOU SHOULDN'T MISS**
ISBN 978-3-95451-649-0

Gordon Streisand
**111 PLACES IN MIAMI
AND THE KEYS
THAT YOU MUST NOT MISS**
ISBN 978-3-95451-644-5

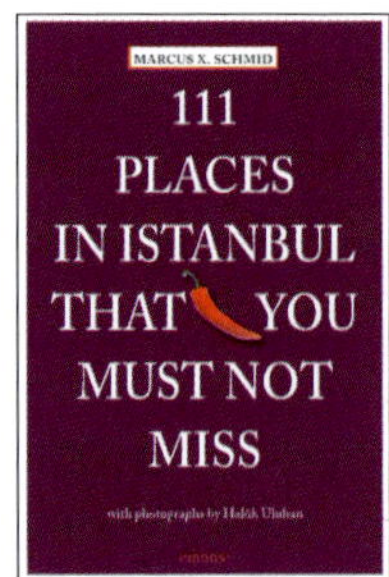

Marcus X. Schmid
**111 PLACES IN ISTANBUL
THAT YOU MUST NOT MISS**
ISBN 978-3-95451-423-6

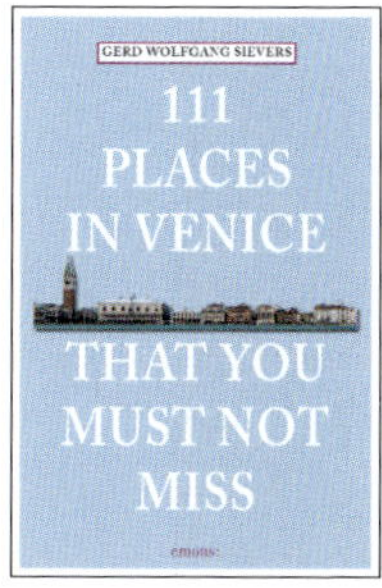

Gerd Wolfgang Sievers
**111 PLACES IN VENICE
THAT YOU MUST NOT MISS**
ISBN 978-3-95451-460-1

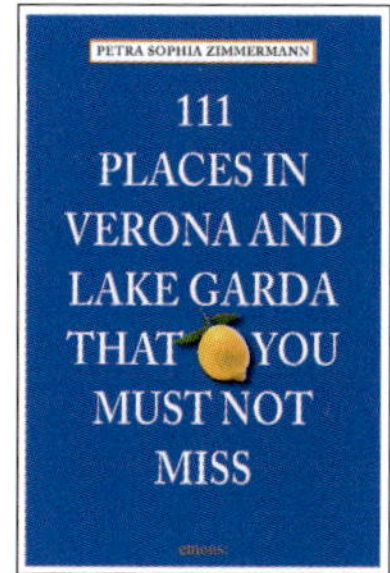

Petra Sophia Zimmermann
**111 PLACES IN VERONA
AND LAKE GARDA THAT
YOU MUST NOT MISS**
ISBN 978-3-95451-611-7

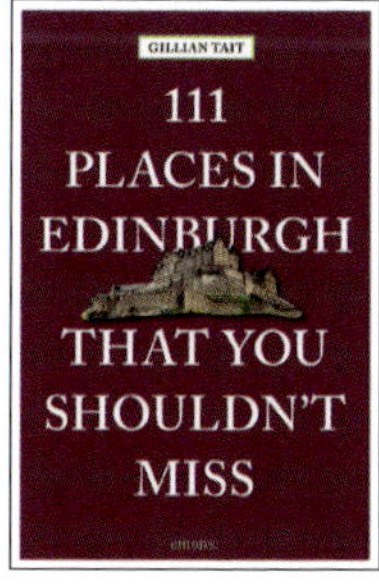

Gillian Tait
**111 PLACES IN EDINBURGH
THAT YOU SHOULDN'T MISS**
ISBN 978-3-95451-883-8

Laurel Moglen, Julia Posey
**111 PLACES IN LOS ANGELES
THAT YOU SHOULDN'T MISS**
ISBN 978-3-95451-884-5

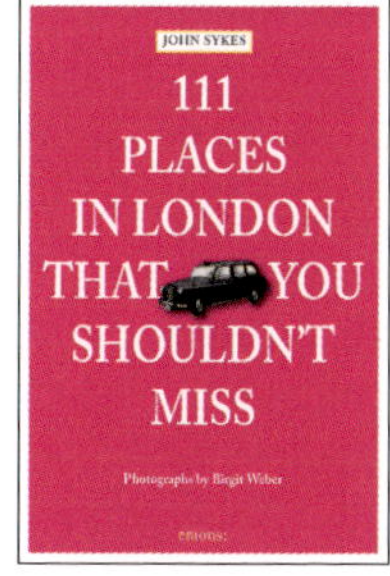

John Sykes
**111 PLACES IN LONDON
THAT YOU SHOULDN'T MISS**
ISBN 978-3-95451-346-8

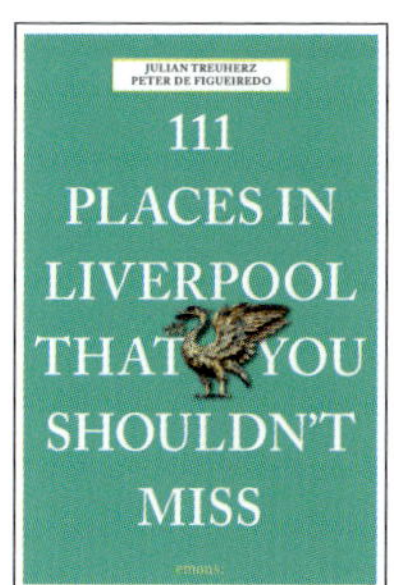

Julian Treuherz, Peter de Figueiredo
**111 PLACES IN LIVERPOOL
THAT YOU SHOULDN'T MISS**
ISBN 978-3-95451-769-5

Annett Klingner
**111 PLACES IN ROME
THAT YOU MUST NOT MISS**
ISBN 978-3-95451-469-4

Kirstin von Glasow
**111 COFFEESHOPS IN
LONDON THAT YOU MUST
NOT MISS**
ISBN 978-3-95451-614-8

Giulia Castelli Gattinara, Mario Verin
**111 PLACES IN MILAN
THAT YOU MUST NOT MISS**
ISBN 978-3-95451-331-4

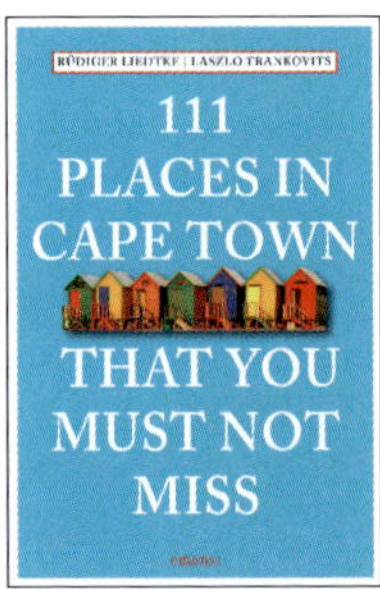

Rüdiger Liedtke, Laszlo Trankovits
**111 PLACES IN CAPE TOWN
THAT YOU MUST NOT MISS**
ISBN 978-3-95451-610-0

Jo-Anne Elikann
**111 PLACES IN NEW YORK
THAT YOU MUST NOT MISS**
ISBN 978-3-95451-052-8

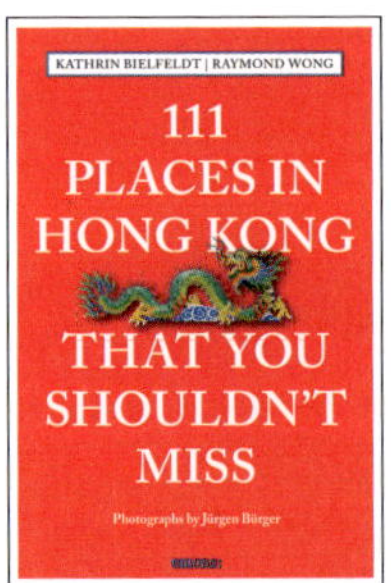

Kathrin Bielfeldt, Raymond Wong,
Jürgen Bürger
**111 PLACES IN HONG KONG
THAT YOU SHOULDN'T MISS**
ISBN 978-3-95451-936-1

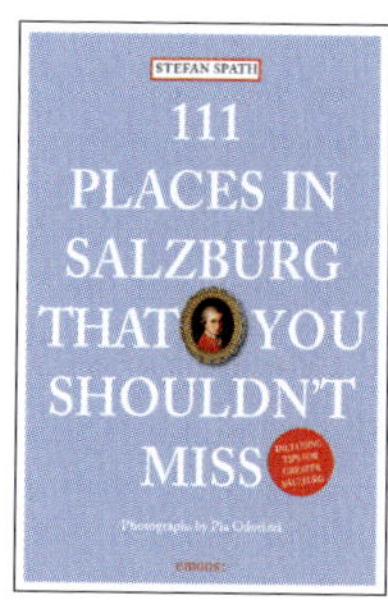

Stefan Spath
**111 PLACES IN SALZBURG
THAT YOU SHOULDN'T MISS**
ISBN 978-3-95451-230-0

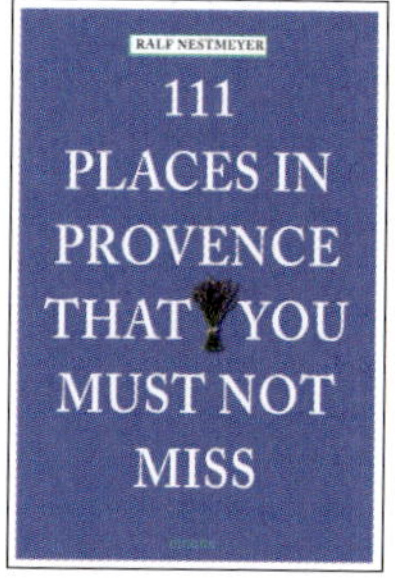

Ralf Nestmeyer
**111 PLACES IN PROVENCE
THAT YOU MUST NOT MISS**
ISBN 978-3-95451-422-9

Beate C. Kirchner
**111 PLACES IN FLORENCE
AND NORTHERN TUSCANY
THAT YOU MUST NOT MISS**
ISBN 978-3-95451-613-1

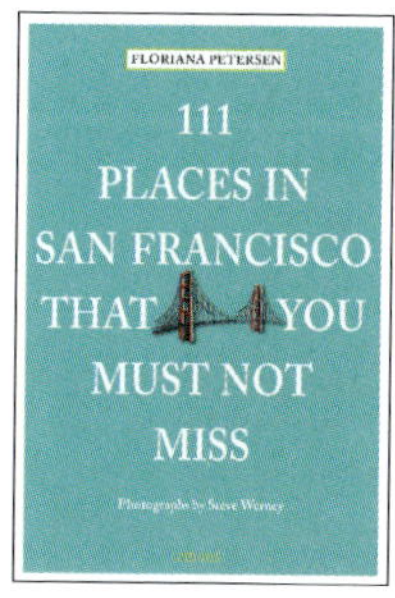

Floriana Petersen, Steve Werney
**111 PLACES IN SAN FRANCISCO
THAT YOU MUST NOT MISS**
ISBN 978-3-95451-609-4

Ralf Nestmeyer
**111 PLACES ON THE
FRENCH RIVIERA
THAT YOU MUST NOT MISS**
ISBN 978-3-95451-612-4

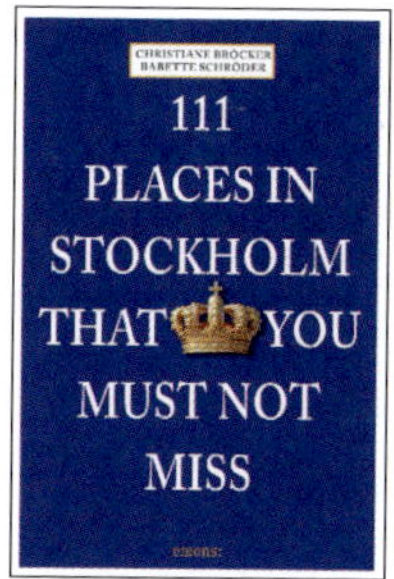

Christiane Bröcker, Babette Schröder
**111 PLACES IN STOCKHOLM
THAT YOU MUST NOT MISS**
ISBN 978-3-95451-459-5

Acknowledgements

We would like to thank Zdeněk Lukeš, Vladimír 51, Alžběta Petři-
nová, Ladislav Čumba and all our friends and acquaintances, without
whose help many interesting places in this book would be missing.

Authors

Matěj Černý was born in Prague, and spent
his childhood and youth until 1989 in his
beloved district of Malá Strana. Today he ex-
plores the whole city, discovering many magical spots outside the tourist ghetto. He studied
journalism and media communication at the
Charles University in Prague, and worked for
the human rights organisation People in Need. At present he earns
a living as an advertising copywriter in Prague.

Marie Peřinová has lived in Prague since 1998.
While studying journalism and politics, she fell
in love with the city at once. She loves secret
passages and long walks through Prague's residential quarters and parks. She has worked for
the NGOs People in Need and Open Society
Fund, with a focus on the problems of human rights and media in
the Czech Republic and worldwide.